THE MID-ATLANTIC TREASURE COAST

THE MID-ATLANTIC TREASURE COAST

Coin Beaches & Treasure Shipwrecks from Long Island to the Eastern Shore

STEPHEN M. VOYNICK

THE MIDDLE ATLANTIC PRESS
Wallingford, Pennsylvania

©1984 by Stephen M. Voynick
ISBN: 0-912608-16-1
Maps prepared by The Bookmakers, Incorporated
Manufactured in the United States of America

Published by
The Middle Atlantic Press
Box 263, Wallingford, PA 19086

Library of Congress Cataloging in Publication Data
Voynick, Stephen M.
   The mid-Atlantic treasure coast.
   Includes index.
   1. Atlantic Coast (United States)—Antiquities.
2. Treasure-trove—Atlantic Coast (United States)
3. Coin hoards—Atlantic Coast (United States)
4. Shipwrecks—Atlantic Coast (United States)   I. Title.
F106.V69   1983   974   82-18846
ISBN 0-912608-16-1

This book is for my mother

It is not the gold so much as the satisfaction of solving the riddle, 'though some gold would do no harm.

Simon Lake, on the salvage of the H.M.S. Hussar
September 26, 1936

Contents

Preface

Growing up along the New Jersey shore meant walking sandy beaches, climbing rolling dunes, and looking seaward, while letting my imagination run as free as the distant ships on the Atlantic horizon. Years later, an interest in marine treasure salvage took me to other coasts, those of the Caribbean and South America, where my shipmates and I found both treasure and adventure—never enough treasure, it seemed, and sometimes too much adventure.

It was treasure salvage that brought me back to the mid-Atlantic coast in 1980, and, off a Delaware beach, our salvage team found still other adventures and more sunken treasure. A curious sense of incongruity between the existence of sunken treasure and the mid-Atlantic coast led me to libraries and archives. There, I found only disjointed accounts of sinkings and salvages, bound loosely together by the strings of embellished legend and lore. Stripping aside the pirate tales and other myths, I discovered the essence of mid-Atlantic sunken treasure to be the legacy of a remarkable history, one reflecting an exciting saga of men and ships simultaneously wonderful and tragic.

I hope this book will encourage at least a few to dive to the remains of a sunken ship, or to seek the rewarding gleam of gold on the sands of a lonely beach. And for those who take their adventure only from the pages of books, perhaps they, too, will find rewards in the accounts of how treasure came to be lost, and found, along the mid-Atlantic coast.

Stephen M. Voynick

INTRODUCTION

Mid-Atlantic Sunken Treasure: The Romance and the Reality

October 11, 1980 ... The Coast of Delaware. Riding easily at its anchors, the barge rose and fell gently with each passing Atlantic swell. From the deck, one could just make out to the south the rising hotels and condominiums of Ocean City, Maryland, and, to the north, the low, irregular outline of New Jersey's Cape May. On the seaward horizon, deceptively tiny silhouettes of great tankers and container ships appeared motionless as migratory strings of brant and scoter winged south over a flat, blue-gray sea. And to the west, the Delaware shore was a long line of churning white breakers backed by rows of rolling, grassy dunes.

Autumn had brought with it a refreshing briskness to the sea air accompanied by the annual return of off-season quietude. Gone were the noisy crowds of summer sunseekers and vacationers, their places taken now by scattered surf fishermen and an occasional wandering beachcomber seeking a treasure of solitude from a lonely sea and beach.

Aboard the barge, men also sought a treasure, but one of a different sort. Throughout the morning, their work had been accompanied by the shrill cry of gulls and the grating whine of electric deck winches. At regular intervals, the sea alongside the barge erupted in a shower of spray as cables retrieved a ponderous clam bucket from the sea bottom forty feet below. The

An industrial barge used in salvage operations off Delaware's coin beach in 1980. The clam bucket operation was seeking gold English guineas from the wreck of the *Faithful Steward.*

bucket dangled on its cable tethers beneath a towering crane, then swung slowly over the deck where the steel jaws disgorged a ton of dripping, muddy sediment. After hoses had washed away the mud and sand, crewmen inspected the remaining material, a collection of broken shells, clams, amorphous pieces of conglomerate, bits of corroded iron, and, in testimony to the enduring efforts of surf fishermen, snarls of monofilament line, sinkers, and rusted hooks.

Nearly every load of sediment yielded thin metallic wafers about the size of a quarter, each encrusted in a green-black layer of corrosion—evidence of centuries of immersion in the sea. The wafers were copper coins, and rubbing revealed images of a bust, a coat of arms, a few words of Latin, and dates from the mid-1700s. They were English and Irish halfpennies, confirming the presence of an ancient shipwreck scattered and buried beneath the sea bottom.

Throughout the morning, while the crane clanked and cables scraped on the deck, the clam bucket probed and sampled the bottom sediments. Each load brought to the surface contained something of interest, at least one copper halfpenny, sometimes several, or perhaps old copper shoe buckles or even a few of silver. By late morning, over one hundred of the copper halfpennies had been recovered. These provided not satisfaction, but merely encouragement, for the object of this search was not the green-black of corroded copper, but rather the brilliant luster of yellow gold.

While the monotony of mechanical dredging off a Delaware beach reflects little of the popular image of marine treasure salvage, what happened next certainly does. Just before noon, gloved hands sorted through yet another load of sediment. Finally, from the jumble of shells and gravel came the long-awaited and unmistakable glint of gold. In a timeless moment, a hand reached into the hopper of dripping shells to retrieve a gleaming gold coin. A chorus of excited voices rose to join the clamor of the gulls and machinery, as the treasure hunters reveled in the shouting, backslapping, and handshaking that is an inherent part of the recovery of lost gold from the sea.

The gold coin was an English Rose guinea, as clean and lustrous as the day it was made. Still dripping with the sea, the coin reflected warm sunlight from its golden features, a stylized royal bust and the elaborate crest of eighteenth century England encircled by Latin words telling of other men in other times:

Aboard the salvage barge, crew members search through debris recovered from the sea bottom. Gold English guineas and hundreds of copper half-pennies were recovered from the shells and gravels.

GEORGIUS III · DEI GRATIA . . . , in English, GEORGE III ·
BY THE GRACE OF GOD · KING OF ENGLAND · 1766.

In the following hours, the sediments yielded more halfpennies, more shoe buckles, and more golden guineas. Gold was
being recovered directly from a Delaware shipwreck for the first
time ever. Ashore, hip-booted surf fishermen watched from the
most steadily productive "coin" or "treasure" beach in the United
States, one where thousands of copper, silver, and gold coins
have been collected over the years. The recovery of sunken gold
from an ancient shipwreck on this October day in 1980 reflected
a growing interest in, and awareness of, the millions of dollars of
sunken treasures that await salvage in the bays and off the
beaches of the mid-Atlantic coast.

Sunken treasure. It would be difficult to find two other words so
steeped in imagery. The sound of the phrase instantly conjures
visions of Robert Louis Stevenson's colorful characters digging
chests of silver on a tropic beach or of divers prowling the ghostly
timbers of a sunken galleon. Sunken treasure is the legacy of that
incredible era of treasure galleons, *conquistadors,* and pirates, and
its traditional and seemingly rightful place is the Spanish Main.
Geographically, sunken treasure has become synonymous with
the Caribbean and the popular stereotype of a modern treasure
salvor is a tanned adventurer in ragged cut-off denim shorts
diving to a shipwreck on a coral reef.

Sunken treasure, by its very nature, has become the most
embellished and exaggerated of all maritime subjects. With every
repetition of a tale, the purported value of a treasure grows, as do
the levels of heroism or hardship attached to the shipwreck or
subsequent salvage attempts. To many, sunken treasure and its
possible salvage is virtually all romance founded on centuries of
legend and lore, all fascinating, but never quite substantiated.
And therein rests much of the current image of mid-Atlantic
sunken treasure: too much romance, too little reality. Besides, it
somehow seems irreverent that sunken treasures worth fortunes
should be located within a few hours driving time of twenty or
thirty million people.

Still, the appeal of sunken treasure is enormous to both active
and armchair adventurers. Very few of us may honestly say we
have never dreamed of diving to an ancient shipwreck or of
finding a silver piece of eight on a beach. Most are content to
let those dreams remain pleasant fantasies, while others con-

template the intriguing and tantalizing possibility of their reality. And so sunken treasure has become a subject divided, part romance, part reality, with both belonging in the distant tropics.

But the gold coins recovered from the Delaware sea bottom that October, 1980, day were real. They were reality as sure and certain as the gleam of the gold itself, confirmation of both the existence of mid-Atlantic sunken treasure and also of a regional maritime history that challenges even that of the Spanish Main for color and excitement.

The mid-Atlantic coast witnessed every aspect of New World maritime history, from the arrival of the first explorers and immigrants to the centuries-long processions of warships, merchantmen, pirates, privateers, and even Spanish treasure galleons. The great ports in New York, Delaware, and Chesapeake Bays brought the heaviest concentration of shipping in the Americas, and the dual hazards of storms and shoals made the mid-Atlantic coast one the most feared graveyards of the Atlantic. Today, as many as 8,000 shipwrecks rest along the mid-Atlantic coast, an estimate based not upon legend, but on actual maritime history, a history that is the basis of both the romance and reality of the sunken treasures of the mid-Atlantic coast.

The following pages are filled with accounts of shipwrecks, coin beaches, and salvages that include—and separate—both the romance and reality of sunken treasure. The shipwrecks and treasures are real, the legends largely imagination, but a rich and colorful part of the lore of the coast. Taken together, they present an exciting and unusual picture of mid-Atlantic maritime history. And since mid-Atlantic sunken treasure is basically a legacy of centuries of shipwrecks, the story should begin with the first ships . . .

PART I

The Mid-Atlantic
Maritime Saga

CHAPTER 1
The New Coast

Whether the first sail to appear off the mid-Atlantic coast was that of a Viking ship about the year A.D. 1000 still remains conjecture. The first documented crossing of the northern Atlantic came only a few years after Columbus had discovered the New World. In 1497, John Cabot, an Italian navigator in the service of England, made a landfall on Canada's Cape Breton Island. His discovery stirred great excitement in London. He sailed west again the following year on one of the most mysterious of all early explorations, a voyage from which neither Cabot nor any of his men ever returned. Some historians believe that John Cabot, or perhaps his son, Sebastian, sailed as far south as the mid-Atlantic coast, but beyond vague mention of forests and promontories unknown, proof does not exist. After two Portuguese navigators sailed to Newfoundland in 1501, European interest and activity in the northern Atlantic waned.

Grand events, however, were taking place to the south, where the Caribbean coast of Latin America was already known as the Spanish Main. Driven by an obsession for gold, the Spanish explored rapidly and, by 1520, had established several bustling, fortified cities. That year, Hernán Cortés led several hundred Spanish soldiers through Mexico in a reckless adventure that paid off in a great golden treasure. In 1524, as the wealth of the broken Aztec Empire was the talk of Europe, a lone ship under the command of Giovanni da Verrazano reached the promontory now known as Cape Fear, North Carolina.

Verrazano, another Italian navigator, had been commissioned by the French to seek a short sea route to the East Indies. After his landfall, he sailed north, noting in his journals, "There appears to me a new land never seen by anyone ancient or modern." Near the present eastern shore border of Virginia and

Maryland, Verrazano entered a barrier beach inlet and anchored, landing an exploration party to venture a short distance into the interior. Continuing north, Verrazano anchored again in New York Bay on April 17, 1524. Prudently concerned about the safety of his single ship, Verrazano had sailed well offshore, so far, in fact, that he completely missed the entrances to Chesapeake and Delaware Bays, which he certainly would have explored as potential passages to the Indies.

From a mariner's standpoint, Verrazano noted precisely the dangers of this new coast. His first concern was the shoaling, which appeared as shifting sand bars near the barrier beach inlets, or as broader shallows lying well offshore. Another disconcerting observation was the absence of any prominent, useful landmarks; the entire coast seemed to be identical barrier beaches and islands, with the eastern shore of Virginia appearing no different from New Jersey. Finally, Verrazano noted that most of the mid-Atlantic coast lay in a north-south direction, and that prolonged northeast onshore winds could potentially drive any ship to destruction on the beaches and shoals.

Even though Verrazano's report contained the first useful description of over one thousand miles of previously unknown coast, it was received with relatively little interest, for European attention remained riveted on developments along the Spanish Main. Only a decade after Cortés had defeated the Aztecs, another Spanish adventurer, Francisco Pizarro, conquered the Incan Empire in Peru, receiving in plunder, ransom, and tribute more gold than Europe had ever seen. Spain suddenly found itself the richest and most powerful nation on earth and the grand era of treasure galleons, doubloons, and pieces of eight was at hand.

Following the Incan conquest, Spain began systematically exploiting the New World riches. Mexican gold and silver was brought to Vera Cruz while South American treasures were accumulated in the Colombian port of Cartagena. From both ports, annual treasure fleets of heavily armed galleons and merchant vessels sailed to Havana, Cuba. There, under protection of the great Morro Castle fortress, the fleets were consolidated and prepared for the long voyage to Spain. Prior to 1550, the east bound treasure fleets plied a dangerous route east from Havana along the northern coast of Cuba, threading their way through the Bahamian reefs to the relative safety of the open sea.

Increased knowledge of winds and currents brought a new route after 1550, one making efficient use of the north Atlantic trade winds and the favorable Gulf Stream current. From Havana, the fleets followed the Gulf Stream through the narrow, reef-lined Straits of Florida, the hazards of which are proven by the many shipwrecks along the Florida coast. After entering the Atlantic, the ships then continued northeast with the Gulf Stream, their final courses dictated by the vagaries of the easterly trades. Spanish New World shipping is most often associated with the Caribbean, but in fact the galleons held the east coast of North America closely, even venturing above 45° north latitude (Halifax, Nova Scotia) before turning east with favorable winds. The fleets often sailed within one hundred miles of the mid-Atlantic coast, vulnerable to the onshore winds of northeast storms.

That Spanish treasure ships wrecked along the mid-Atlantic coast is not questioned, only their number and location. The homebound Spanish fleets sailed this northern route for over 250 years. Until the early 1600s, there existed not a single mid-Atlantic settlement to witness a wreck. Ships and even whole fleets were driven ashore to be pounded to bits in the crashing breakers. Under such conditions, entire crews could have been lost; survivors would have been stranded on inhospitable barrier islands, probably to perish later. Over ten Spanish wrecks have been documented along the mid-Atlantic coast, and it is highly probable that others went unrecorded.

Although sunken treasure can take many forms, its classic definition would always be the cargos of the treasure galleons. The earliest galleons carried gold mostly as small discs and bars, the form preferred to facilitate taxation, accounting, and valuation. By the mid-1600s, gold coins minted in the New World became a regular part of the treasure shipments. The familiar doubloon was an eight *escudo* piece weighing about one ounce. Spanish gold coins were also struck in fractional denominations of one, two, and four *escudos*. A substantial amount of gold was manufactured and shipped as jewelry to cleverly avoid taxation, since gold worn as such upon debarkation in Spain was not subject to the crown "fifth." Spanish gentlemen and soldiers of rank carried their personal gold as "money chains," with each link conveniently weighing one ounce. Such chains were often many feet long and weighed several pounds. As jewelry they were absurd, but as tax evasion gimmicks, they served their owners well.

Cleaned Spanish silver "cobs." These irregularly shaped coins were common until the introduction of round, milled coinage in the mid-1700s. These are pieces of two and one, fractional denominations of the piece of eight.

Silver was shipped in huge tonnages, cast as heavy bars or minted into coins. The eight *reale* silver coin, the celebrated "piece of eight," has become the enduring symbol of treasure and the Spanish Main. Because of disastrous economic management, the gold and silver of Spain and Portugal quickly passed to the rest of Europe, with each nation minting its own coinage. The Spanish doubloon and piece of eight, the Portuguese "Johanna," and later the English guinea were accepted world-wide as legal tender and could be found in varying quantity on most colonial period ships. Today, they are among the more common forms of treasure recovered from colonial shipwrecks.

Well over a century after Columbus had discovered the New World, the barrier beaches of the mid-Atlantic coast remained known only to a handful of explorers. The last important exploration of the coast was made by Henry Hudson in the *Half Moon* in 1609, on a voyage that took him into Delaware and New York Bays and a considerable distance up the river that now bears his name. The marine exploration of the mid-Atlantic coast had been concluded; now other men in other ships would initiate the business of settlement and development. History had already made its first deposits of sunken treasure along the coast, and now the shoals and beaches waited for more.

Two corroded silver Spanish pieces of eight, the popular eight reale coin. The black covering of silver sulfide is normal for silver coins found in the sea, but the cross and shield are still visible.

CHAPTER 2
Brave Men . . . Frail Ships

The dubious niche in history of being the first documented
mid-Atlantic wreck was claimed by a Dutch ship in 1620. Although preceded by others unrecorded, that unfortunate ship
heads a list of thousands of wrecks caused not only by storms and
shoals, but also by primitive navigation and the deplorable
condition of the ships themselves.

Considering the rigors of the trans-Atlantic voyage, the earliest ships were suprisingly small and fragile. Hudson's *Half Moon*,
manned by a crew of seventeen, was only seventy-five feet long
and rated at eighty tons, the size of a modern day-trip party
fishing boat. Early hulls were bulbous, with inordinately deep
drafts relative to length, a configuration often proving disastrous
on Caribbean reefs. Mid-Atlantic sand shoals would not neces-
sarily hole a hull, but the deep drafts meant a grounded ship
would usually remain so. The basic hull fragility was a product of
the era's limited technology in design, construction materials,
and maintenance techniques. Newly constructed hulls quickly
weakened with lack of effective bottom paints, preservatives, and
sheathing. Toredo worms dramatically shortened the working
lives of ships in Caribbean service. Although the wood-devouring
marine worms were not indigenous to the mid-Atlantic, colonial
ships regularly visited the Caribbean, bringing the worms back
with them. Even in calm seas, grounding of a weakened hull
brought separation of seams in wave and tidal action. When
leakage surpassed the capacity of the crude pumps, or if winds
were onshore, disaster was inevitable, for the wooden hulls were
no match for the destructive power of the sea. If shoaled in a
severe northeast storm, even the sturdiest hulls would break up
in a matter of hours.

Poor manueverability and tacking ability created other hazards.
Early ships carried as many as ten anchors rigged for instant

deployment, the last hope to keep off shoals when currents or unfavorable winds precluded steering clear. Canvas sails and the hemp line used for both rigging and anchor cables were subject to rot, and in the stress of storms—the very times they were needed most—they frequently failed. A seventeenth century trans-Atlantic voyage often required eight weeks and was enormously taxing to the health of seamen and passengers. Salting and pickling were the only methods of preservation, and food, stores, and water not already infested with insects and vermin spoiled rapidly. Bad food and deficiencies stemming from imbalanced diets could so debilitate crews that they were unable to handle ships in calm conditions, much less in storms or other emergencies.

If the dangerous coast and fragile ships were not enough, early mariners were further faced with the errors and inaccuracies of the then neophytic science of navigation. Sun measurement and the magnetic compass, both used before the time of Columbus, remained the primary means of navigating for 250 years after the discovery of the New World. The magnetic compass enabled a navigator to determine direction relative to a variable and then mysterious "magnetic north." The use of cross staffs and quadrants to measure the angle of the sun at its zenith off the horizon provided remarkably accurate latitudes, the point between the equator and either geographic pole.

Early coastal navigation charts were based upon compass and sun measurements, visual impressions and interpolations, and a good bit of admitted guesswork. Improvement and refinement of mid-Atlantic charts were greatly hindered by the lack of prominent landmarks to serve as cartographic reference points; for 150 years, even the best charts offered only vague indication of coastal features. Veteran navigators used those charts only as a general reference, wisely placing their faith—and lives—on soundings and the eyes of the lookouts to detect a nearing coast before the ominous rumble of breakers was heard.

Scholars and mathematicians had long known that longitude, or relative east-west position, could be calculated from star positions, given the accurate time. Accordingly, accuracy in both chartmaking and navigation was advanced tremendously after the first practical and reliable shipboard chronometers were introduced about 1730. By 1750, the chronometer and sextant were a part of every Atlantic navigator's instruments.

Post-Revolutionary War charts accurately depicted mid-At-

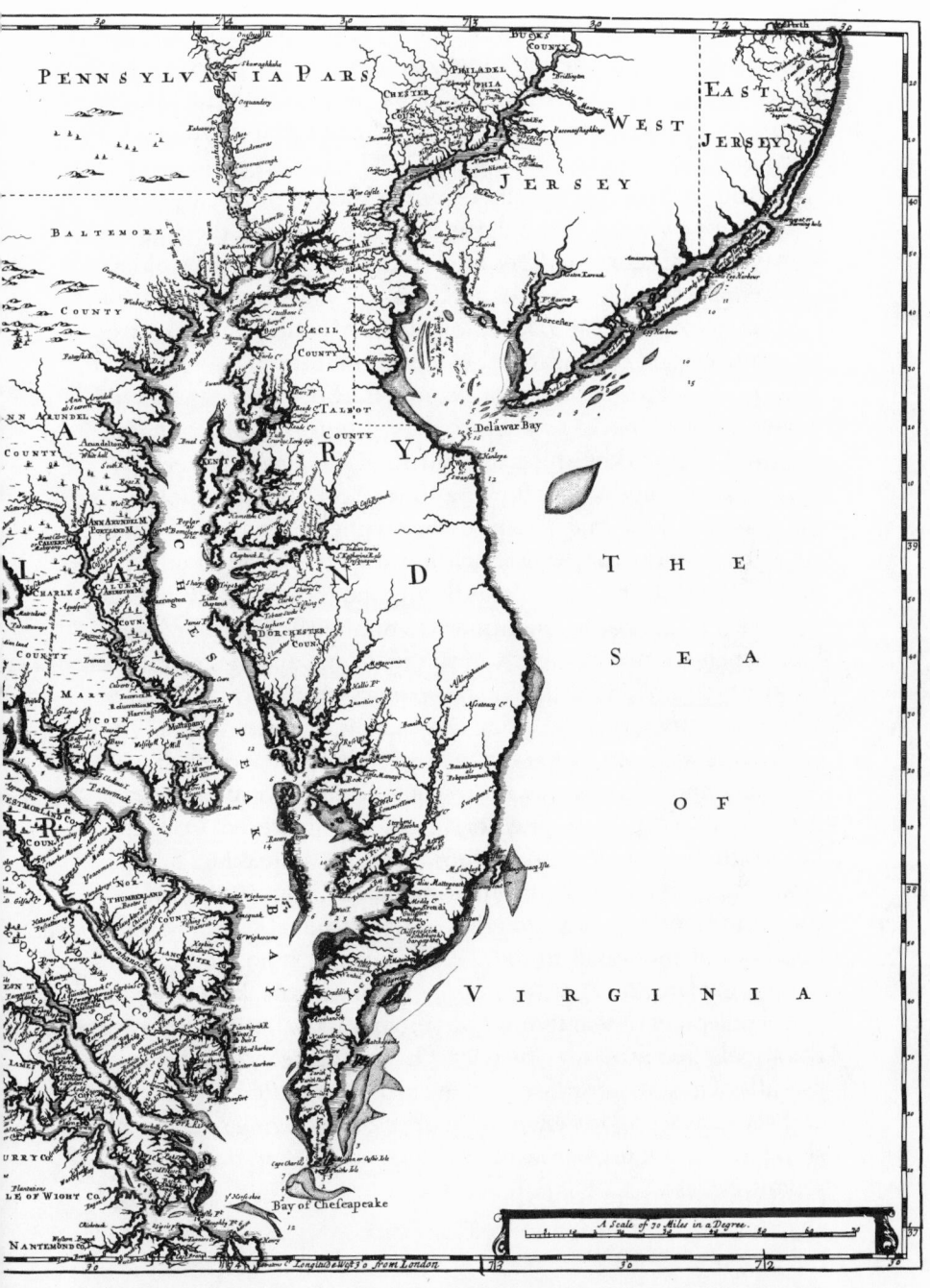

This chart, published about 1719, is improved over previous maps in coastal detail but still exhibits significant longitudinal distortion. Courtesy Mariners' Museum, Newport News, VA.

lantic coastal features, but were totally lacking in sounding data. The depth measurements, which could be taken only with the slow and laborious use of sounding weights, were included only in inner harbor charts of major ports. Charts were sometimes outdated before they were even printed, through rapid and dramatic alteration of coastal features. Violent northeast storms could cut new inlets through the barrier beaches; if the cuts survived tidal action and became established, the nearby older charted inlets could silt over and, in a few years, seem as if they had never existed at all. The colonial era, of course, had no coastal reclamation and stabilization projects, and storms also altered the seaward shoal formations, thus compelling even the most experienced local pilots to venture out cautiously while sounding continuously to determine the course of the new channel.

In the two centuries following Verrazano's voyage, thousands of ships sailed the mid-Atlantic coast without benefit of a single aid to navigation, for the first lighthouses did not appear until the mid-1700s. After a trans-Atlantic voyage, these ships found the approach to the coast a nightmare in poor visibility or darkness. Sail was shortened, the bottom sounded, and anchors readied as lookouts strained to see or hear breakers in time to steer clear. When northeast onshore winds forced ships to reef sail and run before the wind, every person on board prayed that enough open sea remained to the west to allow time for the storm to expend itself. Too often, those prayers were never answered. Driven before the tempests the tiny ships came, seams leaking, pumps straining, sails and rigging in tatters. Finally, above the shriek of the wind came the most dreaded sound imaginable. It was the deep roll of thunder—thunder that came not from the sky, but from great breakers crashing upon unseen shoals. Fear filled the eyes and voices of seamen and passengers as the hull first scraped the shoal, then grounded heavily. The ships careened sickeningly as walls of green water cascaded over the deck, timbers shattered, and screams were drowned in the roar of the raging sea; another ship had completed her last voyage and arrived on the mid-Atlantic coast.

CHAPTER 3
The Graveyard Fills

The Spanish Main had existed for over a century before
mid-Atlantic settlement began in the early 1600s. Hopeful of
emulating the Spanish success in acquiring gold, the first English
settlers also prospected for the precious metal. Captain John
Smith actually shipped back to London for testing promising
mineral samples from Virginia, only to be disappointed. Although the English would never find gold in the mid-Atlantic
region, the endless stream of ships to soon appear would assure
the coast its full share of sunken treasure.

By 1630, English and Dutch settlements were centered around
New York, Delaware, and Chesapeake Bays where the potential
of the protected, deep water harbors as major trade centers was
already recognized. Meanwhile, in Europe, the lure of religious
freedom and the alternative to the depressed Old World economies and societies turned many people toward emigration, eager
to book passage on the growing Atlantic merchant fleet. With the
best of hopes and the worst of fears, these immigrants trusted
their lives to the skill of the navigators and the questionable
seaworthiness of their small ships. Most made the voyage successfully, but for some, arrival in America was tragic. Crowded
together in pitiful steerage accommodations, the unfortunate
ones could only wait helplessly as storms drove the ships onto the
shoals. Unable to make it through the thundering surf, many died
within sight of the land they had crossed an ocean to reach. Their
permanent place in America was found quickly, in one of
the shallow, common graves along the lonely mid-Atlantic
barrier beaches.

Maritime trade was the dominating influence upon colonial
culture and its economy and was first shaped by a fierce English-
Dutch rivalry. Amsterdam, then the greatest port in the world,

profited the Dutch enormously as the transshipment point for nearly all European imports and exports. After developing a strong navy in the late 1600s, England challenged the Dutch shipping supremacy through a complex series of trade regulations known collectively as the Navigation Acts. Colonial imports could now come only from England and only on English ships, thus forcing colonial merchants to adopt new trade routes. Fish, flour, and lumber from the colonies were shipped to the West Indies and exchanged for sugar, molasses, and other tropical products for shipment to England. The last leg of this long, circuitous voyage brought English manufactured and transshipped good back to the colonies. Deep resentment over the Navigation Acts would eventually lead to revolution, but manifested itself immediately in the formation of a large mid-Atlantic smuggling industry. The numerous coves in the large bays and the tricky barrier beach inlets were well suited for smuggling and made the practice impossible to control. For a man with a small ship and the willingness to accept a bit of risk, colonial smuggling was a direct and quick way to a small fortune.

New York, Philadelphia, and Baltimore grew rapidly into leading ports and centers of population and development. Between them, however, the long sections of coast remained wild and unsettled. As late as 1700, shipwreck survivors faced terrible ordeals of isolation and starvation on the remote barrier islands. Along the eastern shore, instances of cannabalism were reported among survivors. Some groups wandered for weeks before stumbling onto help, usually from friendly Indians.

By the late 1600s, shipping had become heavy enough to make lucrative the most notorious of all maritime practices—piracy. In the Americas, piracy began as what many considered a highly patriotic endeavor. A legion of English buccaneers, Drake and Morgan foremost among then, harassed the Spanish everywhere to capture fortunes from treasure fleets and ports. While amassing great personal wealth, they were received as heroes in England. The pirates, however, soon abandoned the point of honor of attacking only Spanish shipping and, now that English ships were becoming victims, London decreed piracy a crime. Criminal or not, many colonial merchants were ambivalent about piracy; even though colonial law punished piracy by hanging, the freebooters were quietly welcomed in most ports as some of the few visitors able to pay for services and supplies with hard cash, that is, gold and silver. Delaware and Chesapeake Bays became centers of piracy; their many coves offered protection and immediate access to the heavily-traveled shipping routes. Both Edward Teach, better known as Blackbeard, and Captain William Kidd, together with a host of lesser-known but equally ruthless pirates, operated from mid-Atlantic bases.

Colonial piracy reached such frightening levels by 1690 that even the staid London Parliament made it a capital offense. Kidd found his final reward at the end of a rope and Teach at the end of a naval cutlass. After that, many pirates wisely took advantage of an offer of general amnesty to retire alive. The peak of colonial piracy had passed by 1720, but the practice, on a lesser scale, lingered on for another century. In their passing, the pirates left a trail of legend and lore second to none. Today, the mid-Atlantic coast has hundreds of pirate tales, a few partially substantiated, but none proven conclusively. Most of the beach recoveries of gold and silver coins are automatically attributed to pirates, but in truth they originate from shipwrecks.

The Revolution brought an influx of British and French warships and a new flag—the Stars and Stripes—to many ships that plied the coast. Among those flying the new American flag were another intrepid group of mariners, the privateers, who found the same features of the coast that so appealed to the smugglers and pirates worked to their advantage also. Even though the major ports fell under British naval control, the privateers operated freely, slipping from bays and inlets in their favorite craft, a shallow draft, sixty-foot brig bearing four to six cannon, to harass and plunder British shipping. Aware they were no match for a patrolling frigate, the privateers relied upon stealth and expert knowledge of local waters to achieve their successes. While lining their own pockets, they provided desperately needed war supplies. Many coastal towns thrived by selling services and supplies to the privateers and disposing of their plunder.

The expanded trade following the Revolution brought more ships than ever to the mid-Atlantic coast; by 1800, New York harbor was handling well over 1,500 ships annually. While shipping increased tremendously, improvement in maritime safety remained stagnant. Chart accuracy and navigation procedures had advanced, but the sailing ships still remained at the mercy of the northeast storms. The colonial era had brought hundreds of shipwrecks to the mid-Atlantic coast, but the nineteenth century would bring thousands.

As shipwreck frequency increased, yet another group arose to lend its color and controversy to the growing history of the mid-Atlantic coast. In the early colonial years, most wrecks were simply allowed to break up; large wrecks would litter the beaches for miles with broken timbers, scattered cargo, and bodies. The first incentive to watch for wrecks was the colonial governmental offer of payment of one pound to anyone giving decent burial to one of the bodies that regularly washed ashore. But as the number of wrecks continued to increase, those living near the barrier beaches looked not at the tragedy, but rather at the opportunity to profit.

Wrecking, or "wracking," in its early spelling, was founded upon practical intentions—simply to utilize wreckage material otherwise going to waste. As the full economic potential became apparent, wrecking developed into a highly competitive free-for-all, dominated by ruthless professionals. When word of "Wreck ashore!" was passed along the beaches, rival groups raced to the site. While there was never proof of the use of false lights to lure ships onto the shoals on dark nights, as practiced by the Hatteras (North Carolina) wreckers, neither did the mid-Atlantic wreckers exhibit much humanitarian concern. Wrecking profits were made not through concern with life, but by taking possession of cargos and wreckage as soon as possible. Jersey wreckers considered themselves somewhat more civilized than their Long Island, New York, counterparts who reportedly would not even wait for a shipwrecked person to expire before cutting off fingers to salvage the rings.

Wrecking was a boon to local coastal economies; stores and auctions disposed of cargos and wreckage, while docks and houses were constructed from salvaged planks and timbers. By the early 1800s, uncontrolled wrecking became such a problem that the government finally took action to help rightful owners retain lawful possession of cargos and also to recoup its own substantial lost import duties. The mid-Atlantic states appointed Wreckmasters to oversee events after a wreck. Only limited success was achieved because of the fierce determination of the wreckers, who viewed their profession as a tradition and a God-given right. With poor communication and difficult access to the beaches, wreckers often had time to strip a wreck to nothing before the authorities arrived.

So great became the number of wrecks that insurance costs skyrocketed and many New York merchants faced bankruptcy

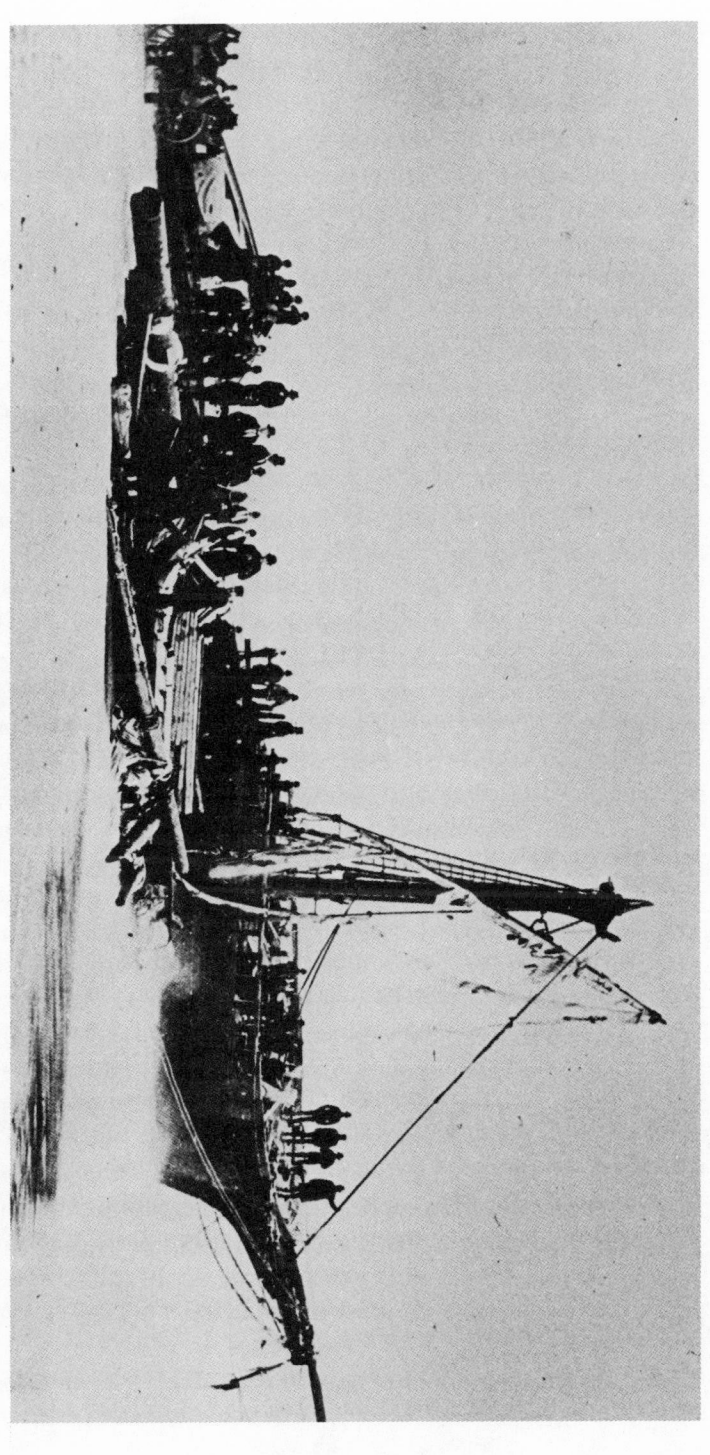

A common scene along the mid-Atlantic beaches in the 1880s. This photo shows organized, legal wrecking of a grounded schooner near Asbury Park, NJ.   Courtesy, *Asbury Park Press.*

with recurring loss of ships and cargos. Today's level of maritime safety makes the comprehension of nineteenth century shipping losses difficult. Consider, for example, that during a stormy two month period in the winter of 1826—27, 200 ships wrecked along the United States Atlantic seaboard. During the 1840s, 158 cargo vessels wrecked on the Jersey shore alone. In spring, 1864, New Jersey's Long Beach Island was the site of 7 wrecks in only thirteen days. An 1877 government report noted 129 wrecks on the eastern seaboard, 40 of them in New Jersey. The winter of 1879–80 was particularly bad and brought 49 more to New Jersey.

In the 1840s, major federal appropriations were made to improve maritime safety. In the late 1700's, the mid-Atlantic coast had only three working lighthouses; construction of others and improvement of existing structures began in earnest in 1842. Equally important was the establishment of a coastal lifesaving service in 1848. Given the condition of most Atlantic wrecks, life-saving in these years was dependent solely upon securing a line to the stranded vessel. This was usually attempted with surfboats from the beach, but in the raging, frigid surf of a northeast storm it was an extremely dangerous job. If surfboat use was impossible, beach crews tried to shoot a line into the ship's rigging. Although many devices were employed for this purpose, the most successful was a carronade-type gun which fired a heavy, rocket-like weight attached to a long line. With a line secured, the business of rescuing seamen and passengers with breeches buoys or metal surf cars could begin.

The early lifesaving crews performed many heroic rescues, but the service became truly professional when it was placed under the Treasury Department's Marine Revenue Service (forerunner of the United States Coast Guard) in 1871. Along the United States coast, 271 Life Saving Stations were established. Eighty were located along the mid-Atlantic coast from Montauk Point, Long Island, to Cape Charles on the eastern shore of Virginia. Hundreds of thousands of lives were saved by the Service from 1871 to 1915, at which time it became a part of the United States Coast Guard.

By 1900, wrecks were still common on the mid-Atlantic beaches, but shipping was well along on its great transition leading to true safety. Steam power, first used in conjunction with sail in the early 1800s, had developed slowly. Early boilers and engines were expensive and unreliable and sail remained the standard system of propulsion for shipping. Increasing numbers of steamers appeared in the 1880s, but "pure" sail schooners, barks, and clippers were still constructed until World War I. Steam power had one incalculable advantage over sail, especially off the mid-Atlantic coast. If sailing room were lost to adverse winds or currents, steamers could easily regain safety offshore, while sailing ships had to fight the centuries-old struggle to keep clear of the shoals and beaches.

Although far safer, steamers were not without problems of their own, mainly the threat of fire and collision. By 1890, steamers were cruising at fifteen knots or more while navigational safety remained dependent upon eyesight and foghorns. In the heavy mid-Atlantic shipping traffic, collisions became more frequent and now steam-powered ships of steel began to join their wooden predecessors on the bottom.

Steel, steam, and diesel power brought unprecedented safety, but other interesting chapters still remained to be written in the history of the coast. World War II brought another rash of sinkings when ships were lost not to the shoals, but to the torpedos of prowling German U-boats. The high level of modern maritime safety became possible after World War II with the introduction of extremely accurate charts, a greatly expanded system of lights and buoys, and an array of electronic instruments that included radar, depth sounders, LORAN, radio direction finders, and, today, even satellite navigation systems. The familiar red-roofed Life Saving Stations have long been put to other use and a beached ship is a rare and newsworthy event. The graveyard reputation of the mid-Atlantic coast could at last fade into history.

CHAPTER 4

Yesterday's History . . . Today's Treasure

Enormous changes have come to some parts of the mid-Atlantic coast since Verrazano's voyage four and one half centuries ago. Surf that once broke unseen upon open beaches now reflects the glare of neon lights and echoes beneath steel piers. Waters once feared and uncharted are sailed by thousands of pleasure boats every summer weekend; further at sea, long, modern steel hulls make their way surely and swiftly through the timeless Atlantic swells. Yet, in striking contrast, there still remain many miles of undisturbed barrier beach where terns nest at the high water line, beach grass waves gently from rolling dunes, and at night the surf breaks only beneath the stars that once guided the early mariners.

If, as they say, the coast could talk, its story would touch every aspect of American maritime history; the story would be of galleons and merchantmen, pirates and privateers, of the men who sailed the ships and the wreckers who waited for them, and of the sweeping transition from frail wooden ships to the steel behemoths of today. In its own way, the coast *does* talk, but only to those who will listen. From time to time, often after one of the storms that once brought tragedy to the beaches, it teases us with a bit of its grand history of men and ships, giving up its story not in words, but rather as some of the treasures it has held for centuries.

Treasure is defined as "a thing of great worth, something rare or precious." Thus, treasure may be tangible or intangible, material or spiritual. The mid-Atlantic coast has both kinds, and they appeal to both realists and romantics. For the realists, the active adventurers who may be divers or treasure hunters, there are the material treasures, the gold, the silver, the historic objects of great value. The romantics will take their treasures from a broader base, perhaps a musket ball, a brass spike, or in the stories of treasure themselves, how it was lost, and how men tried later to recover it. All treasure hunters, whether realists or romantics, and especially the fortunate few who are both, will find the mid-Atlantic coast a rich hunting ground.

Several reasons account for the current interest in the subject of sunken treasure. The first is that its existence may no longer be questioned; the recent, numerous Caribbean recoveries have proven that treasure, the galleons that once carried it, and much of the legend that surrounds it, are quite real. Today, a better educated public enjoys a correspondingly higher level of historical appreciation and awareness. Sunken treasure *is* history, expressed in a manner more effective and exciting than is possible in any textbook. Most knowledge of Spanish colonial maritime history today may be attributed directly to the great publicity that has accompanied the salvage of sunken treasure. The promise of more and richer recoveries to come keeps interest at a high pitch, for advanced electronic and mechanical technology now permits salvors to go after wrecks which, twenty years ago, were beyond their reach.

The most important reason for the interest in sunken treasure is that never before have the objects of treasure been valued so highly. Both gold and silver—the stuff of "classic" treasure— have increased dramatically in price and are now worth ten times their value a decade ago. The bullion price increases have been accompanied by equally sharp rises in numismatic values and, thanks to a heightened appreciation of history, a substantial rise in the artifact value of virtually any historic object recovered from the sea.

In 1948, twenty-six gold coins dating from the mid-1700s were found on a New Jersey beach. Then, the price of gold was fixed at $35 per Troy ounce with correspondingly low numismatic and artifact values. The worth assigned to each of those "pirate" coins, as they were called, was about $75, double the bullion value of the contained gold in a mild concession to age and rarity. The entire recovery was worth about $2,000. Today, only thirty years later, a similar recovery would be worth in excess of

Opposite page: Recoveries from shipwrecks in the mid-Atlantic include such items as lead musketballs, square bronze nails, copper hull sheathing, sheave hubs, and bronze spikes.

$100,000—and *that* is treasure. On a larger scale, the loss of "a million dollars in gold" in the year 1800 meant that about two tons of the metal had gone down with the ship. Today, the bullion value of that same "million" has grown to $20 million; depending upon the form of the gold, current numismatic and artifact values would easily double that figure.

Most ships that wrecked on the mid-Atlantic coast before 1900 carried gold and silver coins, not as treasure cargos, of course, but in smaller quantities for general trading and payroll purposes. Over the years, great quantities of these now very valuable coins were lost in wrecks. But sunken treasure goes beyond gold and silver, for objects of brass, bronze, pewter, crystal, glass, and ceramics, considering their age, rarity, and circumstance of loss and recovery, also qualify as true treasure.

The type and amount of sunken treasure to be found along any coast may be traced directly to local maritime history. And that of the mid-Atlantic coast is perhaps the richest and most varied of all—and so are the treasures that wait in the bays and off the beaches.

PART II

New Jersey Treasures

CHAPTER 5

The Jersey Shore

The Jersey shore stretches 127 miles from Sandy Hook to
Cape May, almost all barrier beach and islands. Strategically
located between New York Bay on the north and Delaware Bay
on the south , the Jersey shore was sailed by more ships over the
centuries than any other similar length of coastline in the
country. Historians estimate that from the early 1600s to the
present, over 4,000 ships came to grief here.

The lore of the Jersey shore is rich in many aspects, but
particularly so in pirate legends. A huge amount of pirate loot is
purported to have been buried along the coast and treasure
hunters have been looking for it a long time, as shown in this
1909 *New York Times* article. (All newspaper articles quoted are
from the *New York Times* unless otherwise noted.)

A SOMERS POINT ROMANCE

Some One Comes Along And Digs Up a Captain Kidd Treasure

ATLANTIC CITY, N.J., February 1.—Somers
Point, in Great Egg Harbor Bay, about ten
miles from this city, is wild with excitement
over the discovery that someone has dug up
and uncovered a brick cave. The supposition
freely heard is that whoever did the digging,
took from there a haul of treasure, greater or
less.

The more romantic are disposed to the

belief that it was money and silver buried by the notorious Captain Kidd, while those of a less romantic temperament think that the treasure recovered was silver plate and gold plate, valuables hidden by residents of Somers Point in Revolutionary days.

The opened cave was discovered this morning not 500 yards from the residence of County Judge E. A. Higbee. There were fresh wagon tracks and the imprint of a long and apparently heavy box or chest in the soft soil. The wagon tracks were followed to the main road that leads to Pleasantville where they were lost.

Mayor John M. Campbell started an investigation, and believes he will be able to learn the identity of the persons who carted away the treasure. Some of the older residents of Somers Point have vivid recollections of persons who have been there looking for Kidd treasure and of at least one person who lost his life in the effort.

This was an Englishman who came to the place with a collection of maps and diagrams, which he carefully guarded from the sight of the curious. He did a great deal of measuring and staking. He attempted to cross the bay one night in a rowboat. The boat was upset and he was drowned. The maps are supposed to have floated away in the swift current, for they were never found.

Somers Point was a seaport in the days of the Revolution, and at times British ships sailed in there. It was believed the ships were sent to rob and plunder the wealthy residents, of which there were many. It is a known fact that many residents did bury their plate, and every reason to believe that many of them never recovered it. It is this which many believe the uncoverers of the cave took away with them . . .

Possibly a rich cache of gold and silver plate was taken from the cave, but the Mayor's investigation failed to determine who the lucky diggers were and the nature of the treasure. Some years later, interest in "pirate" treasure stirred again, this time in Cape May, where plans were made for a salvage expedition.

SEEK PIRATE CRAFT'S GOLD
Cape May Folk Think Old Spanish Hulk Contains $5,000,000

CAPE MAY, N.J., April 25, 1922.—A syndicate is being formed in this city to try to recover $5,000,000 in Spanish gold said to be in the hold of a Spanish vessel that went ashore nearly a century ago on the bar just off Turtle Gut Inlet, at the northern end of Two Mile Beach, about seven miles north of here. The vessel, manned by pirates, was driven off the Spanish Main and was wrecked in a gale. At low water part of the craft is visible.

In the Eighties, Captain George Hildreth, of the Cold Springs Life Saving Station, formed a company to try to recover the gold, but for lack of capital the project was abandoned.

As happens to many dreams of recovering treasure, this one faded away before it really began. But the dream was back in the news again in 1926.

DIGS FOR PIRATE'S HOARD
Burlington (N.J.) Woman Seeks Proof of Blackbeard Legend

BURLINGTON, N.J., October 7.—A century old legend, telling how the pirate Blackbeard buried his plunder beneath an old black walnut tree as a marker, has gained so much credence that Miss Florence E. Steward of Trenton directed a group of laborers in digging for the treasure on her property . . .

According to tradition, Blackbeard buried a Spaniard upright over the treasure chest,

then sailed away never to return. In the
course of time, the walnut tree on Miss
Steward's property became known as "The
Pirate Tree".

The following day, a grisly, however fitting, discovery heightened
the excitement.

FINDING OF HUMAN SKULL SPURS HUNT FOR PIRATE BLACKBEARD'S BURIED TREASURE

BURLINGTON, N.J., Oct. 8.—A human
skull unearthed by school children today
gave renewed zest to the hunt for buried
treasure . . .

Believing the skull might be that of the
Spaniard whom Blackbeard is supposed to
have buried over the treasure, Miss Steward
asked police to guard her property against
further digging by volunteers until she can
personally supervise the work of her own
excavators.

The children found the skull, along with
fragments of other bones, in the corner of an
excavation recently made by workmen. The
report persists that these workmen pried a
large, heavy object and took it with them
when they quit work two days ago . . .

There was never confirmation of the existence of the unseen
chest, and Burlington quieted down when further excavation
revealed no treasure. No treasure was found, but the legends
remained very much alive.

The construction of the Garden State Parkway, a superhigh-
way serving the length of the Jersey shore, aroused hope that the
massive excavations might confirm some of the legends by
uncovering genuine treasure. But the removal of millions of tons
of dirt in prime pirate country brought only disappointment
in 1954.

No Pirate Gold Bared

JERSEY PARKWAY EXCAVATIONS A BLOW TO KIDD LEGEND FANCIERS

RED BANK, N.J., March 26.—No trace of any of Captain Kidd's buried treasure was unearthed during excavation work for the 165 miles of the Garden State Parkway, authorities of the New Jersey Highway Authority reported today.

The announcement was disappointing for many inquirers who thought some of the legendary pirate gold might turn up. The highway parallels the Jersey shore where Kidd was said to have made lengthy visits.

One Monmouth County property owner insisted on reserving his claim to any buried treasure turned up on a parcel of his land that had been used in Parkway construction . . .

The legends of pirate gold appear, fade, and reappear in other versions. The pirate legends of the Jersey shore will endure forever, drawing their permanence from a number of real treasure shipwrecks waiting to be salvaged, and from the gold and silver coins that have been found on Jersey beaches in quantities great enough to warm any pirate's heart.

CHAPTER 6
The Wreck of the Bark Sindia

With the dawn of the twentieth century came the twilight of the great age of sail. Beneath their majestic spreads of billowing canvas, the tall ships still sailed the sea lanes, but in the wakes of the newer, faster steamers. Coastal and trans-Atlantic commerce had been won over to steam power, and a growing fleet of less romantic but infinitely more reliable ships sailed on precise schedules regardless of winds and currents. It was only on the longest voyages, the China trade, that sail still maintained supremacy. Such voyages took a ship halfway around the world; steamer profits were minimized by high coal costs and limited cargo capacity, and the China trade was profitable only to the last of the clippers and great barks.

One such ship was the *Sindia,* a steel-hulled bark designed for cargo capacity rather than outright speed, and one of the largest and finest ships ever built in Belfast, Ireland. The *Sindia* was 330 feet long with a forty-five foot beam and was registered at nearly 3,000 net tons. After her launching in 1887, she logged a quarter million miles on regular runs between her home port of Liverpool, England, and Calcutta, India.

In 1900, the *Sindia* became the flagship of the Anglo-American Oil Company and began service from New York. She left that port on what was to be her last voyage in January, 1901, bound for Shanghai, China. After discharging her cargo of oil at Shanghai, she proceeded to Kobe, Japan, to take aboard a full cargo of silks, fine Japanese porcelain, camphor, linseed oil, and matting for shipment to New York. Departing Kobe in late July, the *Sindia,* with Captain Alex MacKenzie commanding a crew of thirty-three, began her 12,000 mile voyage. After crossing the Pacific, the *Sindia* beat around Cape Horn, then turned north through the Atlantic on the last leg of her voyage.

Just after midnight on Sunday morning, December 15, 1901, the *Sindia* was only fifteen hours out of New York and fighting her way through a nor'easter off the southern New Jersey coast. Poor weather had prevented accurate determination of position and, for several days, the ship had proceeded by "dead reckoning," an approximation of position derived from known direction and estimated speed and one often subject to considerable error, especially in storm conditions. About midnight, lookouts were relieved to see a steady light to the west. They informed the watch officers, who erroneously judged it to be one of the New York lights. When that judgement was made, the fate of the ship was effectively sealed. The *Sindia* continued north until 2:00 A.M., then course was altered to the west, all aboard believing the ship was in the approaches to New York Bay. The light upon which that premise was based had not been a New York light, but the Cape May Lighthouse. This was an error other ships had made, for in these years, most lights showed only a steady beacon, not the modern identifying flash sequences. As Captain MacKenzie slept, his ship raced before a blizzard bound for destruction. Within minutes, the *Sindia* ran onto the shoals 150 yards off the beach at Ocean City, New Jersey.

Her distress signals were answered by the Middle and Ocean City Life Saving Stations. Lines were fired into the rigging of the *Sindia,* only to chafe through and part as the great steel hull heaved and worked its way deeper into a sandy grave. The storm still raged undiminished at dawn and Ocean City residents over

The bark *Sindia* grounded and holed at Ocean City, NJ, December, 1901. Courtesy Ocean City Historical Museum.

one mile from the site awoke to what seemed to be the sound of
cannon. As word spread of "Wreck ashore!" hundreds gathered
at the beach to learn that the thunder was the sound of great sails
being torn to shreds on the yards. Life Saving crews heroically
managed to reach the *Sindia* in surfboats. By late morning, the
last man, Captain Alex MacKenzie, was safely brought to
the beach.

On December 18, the *Sindia* headlined the maritime obituary
in the *New York Times.*

BARK SINDIA A TOTAL LOSS
CARGO OF JAPANESE SILKS GONE

OCEAN CITY, N.J., Dec. 17.—The bark
Sindia, which came ashore on Sunday morning in the storm, as she was working up the
coast toward Sandy Hook, the end of her long
voyage from Kobe, Japan, will never float
again. She broke in two amidships today and
she is a complete wreck.

The cargo, which is entirely lost, consisted
largely of silks, satins, and Japanese wares
which were ruined by the water before the
ship broke. When the vessel hit, she stove a
hole in her bow, and within a few hours there
were nine feet of water in the hold. This
morning there were twenty-four. The wreckers left her this morning, it being useless and
highly dangerous to work on her while the
sea remained as it did. They predicted that
she would begin to break up in a few hours,
as the incessant pounding had started her in
every part.

The *Sindia* was taken charge of by the underwriters who had
insured her $1,200,000 cargo for half its value, and the United
States Customs Service maintained a watch on the wreck. In final
tribute to her seaworthiness, the *Sindia* did not break up; the
steel hull merely worked its way deeper into the sand. The
underwriters soon sold the wreck and the cargo to the newly
formed Sindia Company for only $5,000. They, in turn, sold it to
another salvage company for double that amount. Divers worked
inside the flooded holds for months but sand and water prevented complete salvage.

During the salvage, a narrow wooden pier was built from the
beach to the wreck and much of the recovered cargo was sold at
the "Sindia Store," a group of tents right on the beach. It was her
fine porcelain cargo that qualified the *Sindia* as a treasure ship. In
her holds were 3,315 carefully packed crates of the finest hand-
painted, exquisitely decorated Japanese porcelain, ranging from
delicate butter dishes to large pitchers, urns, and vases. Divers

managed to salvage only about 1,000 crates. These were broken
open and their contents sold on the beach at prices as low as ten
cents for smaller pieces and only two dollars for large, three-foot-
high vases.

The final chapter of the *Sindia* tragedy took place in spring,
1902, when a British Admiralty Court of Inquiry found Captain
MacKenzie and his officers guilty of negligence. MacKenzie, his
will broken, lived but six months more. Salvage was finally halted
in the spring when progressive settling of the hull put the decks
constantly awash. Stripped now even of her masts, the rusting
hulk still worked deeper with each northeast storm. Today, eight
decades after the *Sindia* ran aground, no map is yet needed
to find her remains; her rudder post and tiller may be seen
above water at low tide just off the Ocean City boardwalk at
Sixteenth Street.

The Ocean City Historical Museum, only one mile from the
wreck site, maintains an outstanding shipwreck and sailing
exhibit aptly named the "Sindia Room," where artifacts, photo-

Sindia china display at the Ocean City Historical Museum, Ocean City, NJ. Two
thousand cases of the fine Japanese porcelain remain aboard the wreck.
Courtesy Ocean City Historical Museum.

graphs, models, and documents relating to the *Sindia* may be seen. The heart of the exhibit is a beautiful collection of fine Japanese porcelain that came within fifteen hours of completing its voyage to New York. A magnificent urn over three feet tall,

OF THE 3000 CASES OF CHINA WHICH WERE PART OF THE SINDIA CARGO ONLY 1000 WERE REMOVED. THE REST LIE UNDISTURBED BY THE HAND OF MAN.

The larger pieces in the *Sindia* china display are valued at well over $1,000 each. Courtesy Ocean City Historical Museum.

identical to those sold at the old "Sindia Store," stands next to a model of the bark. Similar porcelain of modern manufacture, if it could be found, would sell for about $1,000 each; accordingly, museum officials hesitate to place a value on their collection. Ocean City residents fortunate to own pieces which have been passed down through families, have turned down very high cash offers. It is tantalizing to think that over 2,000 cases of porcelain remain aboard the *Sindia*. Sand scouring might have ruined it, but the *Sindia* did not break up and the porcelain is still packed in its original shipping crates deep in the sand filled holds.

Many people pause on the Ocean City boardwalk to look out at the rusted rudder post, all that remains to remind them of the once great *Sindia*. Some think of the raging storm when the bark grounded, others think of the fine Japanese porcelain now worth over one million dollars still waiting to be unloaded.

CHAPTER 7

The Foundering of the Spanish Frigate Juno

By 1802, Spain faced bankruptcy as she vainly fought the waves of independence sweeping her once glorious New World colonies. The ports of Cartagena, Colombia, and Vera Cruz, Mexico, now shipped just enough treasure to keep the failing economy afloat. The last of Spain's New World silver was no longer shipped aboard the great lumbering galleons, but was now consigned to swifter, well-armed naval frigates.

Two such frigates, the thirty-four gun *Juno* and the forty gun *Anfitrite,* each carrying a consignment of over ten tons of Mexican silver, departed Vera Cruz in January, 1802, home bound for Spain. Both ships soon suffered mast and rigging damage in rough weather. Rather than attempt the long Atlantic crossing without repairs, course was altered for San Juan, Puerto Rico. After repairs, they remained in San Juan to await arrival of a troopship with a home bound Spanish infantry battalion from Africa. Rather than beat against wind and current up the African coast, it was faster to cross the south Atlantic before the wind, then transfer the troops to eastbound ships that would seek the easterly trades of the north Atlantic. The *Juno* and *Anfitrite* finally departed San Juan on October 1, 1802, with nearly 1,000 passengers, seamen, and soldiers crowded aboard.

One week later, at 33° north latitude, roughly that of Bermuda, worsening weather separated the two frigates. The *Juno,* under command of Captain Don Juan Ignacio Bustillo, hove to for several days hoping the seas would subside and the winds would become favorable, then resumed her northerly course to reach the trade winds. Beneath gray skies, the *Juno* sailed alone, pitching and rolling through the long Atlantic swells, with those

aboard reconciled to a most unpleasant voyage. Like other
frigates of the period, the *Juno* was not particularly large; although only about 170 feet long, 431 people were jammed
together in her damp, wretched quarters.

Day after day, the *Juno* wallowed heavily in the face of stiff
northeast winds that permitted progress only to the northwest.
On October 22, three weeks out of San Juan, gale winds damaged
a mast and carried away the mainsail. Below decks, a far more
serious problem was developing. Hull seams were opening; by
morning, the watch reported six feet of water in the hold.

October 23 was devoted solely to pump maintenance and hull
repair. The worst separation and leakage was forward, and in an
effort to raise the bow, the anchors were cut loose and heavy
equipment and cargo moved aft. Half the ship's guns, all those
forward of the mainmast, followed the anchors into the gray
Atlantic. Below decks, caulking was hammered into seams and
planks were coated with liberal applications of pitch. Seamen and
soldiers sweated and cursed side by side on the heavy pumps,
their best efforts only slowing the rise of seawater in the hold.
Sails were secured over the outside of the hull in a last desperate
hope of controlling the leaks, but the continual heaving of the
water-logged frigate only opened other seams.

The next morning, gray light revealed the welcome sight of a
distant sail. It was the American schooner *Favorite,* which recognized the distress flags of the *Juno* and stood by. Through signals,
Captain Bustillo informed the American of the nature and
seriousness of his plight; in reply, the *Favorite* signaled it would
continue to stand by should abandonment become necessary.

On October 25, the *Juno* sent a launch across the heavy seas to
the schooner. Aboard was Lieutenant Francisco de Clemente and
six other officers whose mission was to assure clarity of signal
communication if the *Juno* were to founder. Escorted by the
schooner, the slowly sinking frigate sailed west to seek refuge in a
United States port. By October 27, the heavy seas had further
weakened the hull, opened more seams, and carried away the
rudder. Bucket brigades joined the weary pump crews and a
makeshift rudder was fashioned. A brief break in cloud cover
allowed an approximate position sight; at noon on the 27th, four
long weeks out of San Juan, the *Juno* had made it above 38° north
latitude and was an estimated 200 miles southeast of Cape May,
New Jersey.

That night, the *Favorite* lost her own mainsail, reducing her speed to an estimated eleven knots. Both ships ran west-north-west with all the canvas they could bear in an apparent effort to make Delaware Bay, but time was against them. About midnight, the *Juno* was seen to be wallowing very low with ten feet of seawater in her hold. The *Favorite* closed distance as much as possible, about "a third of a cable," or 200 feet, close enough to hear the cries for help from the hundreds of panic-stricken Spaniards on the deck of the *Juno*. After that, the storm separated the ships and contact was never re-established.

The morning of the 28th brought dramatically improved weather with cool, clear air and the wind coming briskly from the west over subsiding seas. The *Favorite* found herself alone on an empty ocean. No sail was seen during a day-long search. Three days later, the *Favorite* anchored in Boston Harbor to report the incident.

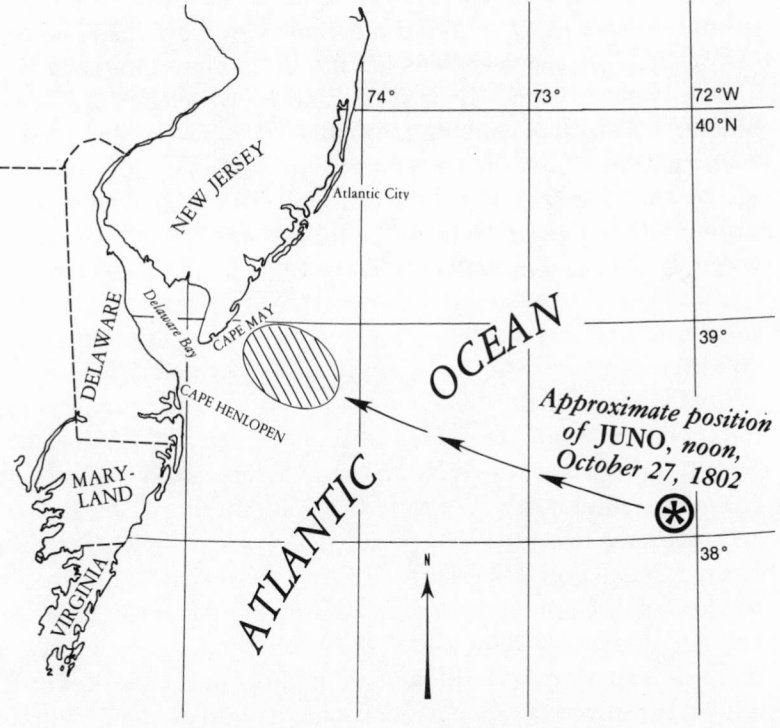

The approximate course of the *Juno* from its estimated position on October 27, 1802, until its sinking the following day. Some authorities believe the wreck site lies within the indicated area off Cape May.

The *Juno* did not reach the beaches, for survivors or wreckage would have been found. The exact location of the sinking, in which all 425 aboard drowned, remains unknown. In the later inquiries, witnesses from the *Favorite* stated their belief that the sinking occurred near the mouth of Delaware Bay and the tip of Cape May. Today, some authorities feel the site is about twenty-five miles east of the mouth of the Bay in ninety feet of water. At least one local salvor who has researched the wreck believes it is much closer and in as little as forty feet of water.

The wreck of the *Juno,* on the continental shelf and within conventional SCUBA range, is well worth seeking. The nature of the sinking—foundering in relatively deep water—assures that the ship went to the bottom intact and probably remains so today. Her timbers have long deteriorated and the site, if it is not buried, may be marked by a characteristic oval pile of ballast rock and a scattering of cannon.

The cargo of the *Juno* was silver; some authorities fix the amount at three hundred thousand ounces, or more than twelve tons. When lost, the value was about four hundred thousand dollars. Today, the increase in silver bullion prices have raised the value of the wreck to about four million dollars, not counting the personal valuables of the passengers or the historic artifacts. The value of the treasure, the workable depth of water, and the intact nature of the wreck site that would facilitate salvage make it very probable that the *Juno* will someday give up her silver fortune.

CHAPTER 8

New Jersey Coin Beaches

HIGHLANDS

The little shore community of Highlands, nestled at the base of
Sandy Hook beneath the Twin Lights of Navesink Highlands,
was abruptly jolted from its off-season tranquility in April, 1948.
The excitement came not from tourists taking advantage of an
early spring, but from locals taking gold coins from the sandy
banks of the Shrewsbury River. William Cottrell, a lobsterman,
together with his father and three friends, chanced to discover a
strange foreign gold coin dating to the mid-1700s. More curious
than excited, they dug further and found another. Finally, when
they had collected eight gold coins, they announced their discovery. What followed confirmed the lure and mystique of treasure,
and the *New York Times* carried the news on its front page.

> ## COINS OF 1770 START GOLD RUSH IN JERSEY
>
> HIGHLANDS, N.J., April 9.—The finding of
> several eighteenth century coins started a
> gold rush here today. Several hundred per-
> sons armed with rakes, picks, and shovels
> scratched and dug on the banks of the
> Navesink River near the place of the first
> discovery . . .

If any potential gold seekers missed those headlines, the *Asbury
Park Press* spread the news up and down the Jersey shore.

HIGHLANDS GOLD RUSH
FOLLOWS COIN DISCOVERY

HIGHLANDS.—A lobster fisherman, his seventy-five year old father and three other rivermen yesterday started a gold rush on the Highlands riverfront when they announced the discovery of eight gold coins of foreign origin, dating to 1735.

Prospectors with shovels and screens, rakes, pails, and nets tore up the Shrewsbury River shore near the foot of Cedar Street until dark last night and had begun search operations before 7:00 A.M. today. Private property owners, at first humored by the expedition, were beginning to ban the gold seekers from their land this morning.

The amazing picture of 300 persons scrounging in the sand moved oldtimers of the Highlands to draw on their pipes and recite the town's history from the time when pirates smuggled riches ashore at, it is claimed, the very spot where sparkling coins have been located this week . . .

Within one day after the start of the gold rush, over two dozen coins had been reported found. Although first thought to be Spanish or French, a coin dealer identified them as Portuguese "Johannas," a one-ounce gold piece named after Portugal's King John whose bust appears on the obverse of the coin. Johannas became common and universally accepted in the eighteenth century when Portugal, after discovery of the rich Brazilian gold fields, minted enormous quantities.

Although the richest concentration of the the coins seemed to be "below the high water mark and on boro property," private property was not spared from the busy shovels, and soon the army of gold seekers, reporters, and curious were joined by the New Jersey State Police.

The north tower of the Twin Lights atop Navesink Highlands, NJ, overlooks the approaches to New York Bay, Sandy Hook, and the town of Highlands.

Jersey Gold Rush Turns to
Comedy as Beach Owners Battle Diggers

HIGHLANDS, N.J., April 11.—A gold hunt that yesterday held all the nervous excitement of a chapter from Stevenson's "Treasure Island" turned into a Mack Sennett comedy today as hundreds of people continued to dig here for Portuguese doubloons.

Clashing in a frenzied "gold war" were property owners and New Jersey State Troopers on one side and eager searchers for loot of eighteenth century buccaneers on the other.

The trouble between the indignant bungalow owners and the self styled privateers began yesterday when the owners, arriving from northern New Jersey when word spread that two dozen gold pieces had been discovered, found their beach fronts looking like they had undergone heavy shelling.

Thirty or forty craters, some of them as much as six feet deep, had been dug in the 300 foot strip of beach where the coins were unearthed. The beach borders the mouth of the Shrewsbury River which in turn empties into Raritan Bay, a favorite hideout for the square-rigged ships of many famous pirates . . .

As fascinating as the gold itself were the countless stories of the supposed origin of the coins, many of which centered about Spermaceti Cove and "the caves on the lower end of the Hook" where human bones believed to be those of pirates (although it is questionable how one might tell the difference) had been found long ago. The gold coins also brought to mind James Fenimore Cooper's famous novel *The Water Witch* telling of a fictional pirate captain who smuggled ashore Old World riches at this very same place.

When the excitement was over, twenty-eight gold Johannas had been reported found; no one knows how many were quietly slipped into pockets. At the time, in 1948, finders refused offers of $30, but found no buyers when they demanded $200 each. Most of the coins that were sold brought $75. Perhaps the Highlands treasure was found thirty years too soon, for each of those gold Johannas is now worth several thousand dollars.

Oldtimers still argue about the coins today, some claiming they were part of buried loot, others believing they came from a shipwreck that still lies buried in the Shrewsbury River channel. It is generally agreed that the coins were dredged up onto the banks in a channel-deepening project some years prior to their discovery, and that there are probably some scattered along the Sandy Hook bank also. Whatever their origin, they probably represent a small part of those still remaining in the sands. Perhaps the oldtimers were right and nearby Spermaceti Cove is the site of buried treasure, or possibly James Fenimore Cooper wrote *The Water Witch* from more than just imagination.

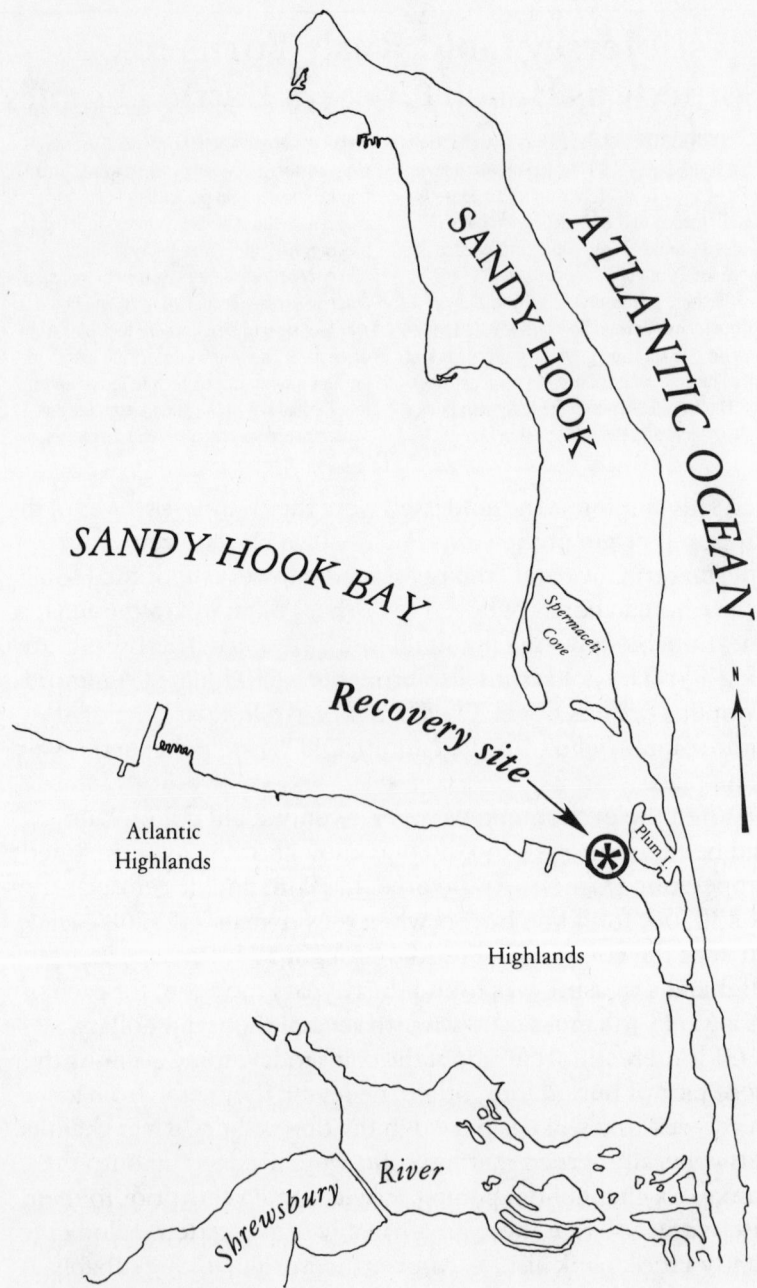

Highlands, NJ, site of the recovery of gold Portuguese Johannas in 1948. The coins are believed to have been dredged from the bottom of the channel between the recovery point and Plum Island, Sandy Hook.

ASBURY PARK

Sometimes, when the sea gives back some of the treasure it has taken from yesterday's ships, the timing can be humorous, as it was with this 1956 incident that occurred near the Asbury Park beachfront amusement center.

COIN HUNT IS HATCHED BY EASTER EGG AFFAIR

ASBURY PARK, N.J., March 29—City Officials preparing to stage an annual Easter egg hunt for children on the beach here Saturday were confronted with the problem of keeping adult treasure hunters away.

Yesterday, Charles Holland, a workman cleaning up the beach preparatory to hiding the eggs, raked up a dozen old Spanish coins. They bore dates ranging from 1760 to 1784 and were about the size of American half dollars. They appeared to be of silver. On one side were the words "Carolus III" and the profile of a male character and on the reverse side the word "Hispana."

The coins are being examined by a local coin dealer to determine their worth. From time to time, similar coins have been found on the beaches in this area, reviving legends about buried pirate loot and sunken treasure.

Beach officials posted a watch at the scene to prevent trampling on the sand before the egg hunt. A number of adults had appeared with digging equipment to seek more of the coins.

The coins of the Asbury Park "Easter treasure" were eight reale silver pieces bearing the image of King Charles III. As is the case with most beach coin recoveries, a northeast storm had "turned over" the sands to uncover the coins. After the children had found their Easter eggs, the beach was declared "open" and the treasure hunters returned to dig with a vengeance. More Spanish silver coins were recovered, but the number was not determined.

POINT PLEASANT

The recoveries of beach coins are poorly documented because of secrecy and excitement, but that was not the case with a gold coin recovery made in Point Pleasant in 1937. The story was reported by the *Asbury Park Press*.

---

65 Rare Gold Coins Found by Howland Worth $8,000

POINT PLEASANT—Sixty-five rare gold coins contained in a dog shaped bank unearthed yesterday by Jesse A. Howland, Seabright jetty contractor, have a value of approximately $8,000 . . .

The contractor who has been in the dredging business 47 years and is an ardent coin collector, found the bank on the banks of the Manasquan-Bay Head Canal where dredging is being done preparatory to building a steel bulkhead.

Howland said the 65 coins date from 1797 to 1877 and were in denominations of $1, $2.50, $3, $5, and $10. Their total denominational value is $1,500.

Recalling that the spot was formerly farmland before the canal came into being, Howland said he believed the coins may have belonged to a retired sea captain.

Eight thousand dollars was a considerable sum in 1937, but the value of the coins today is far greater. All were United States gold coins; considering their age and the numismatic rarity of some dates, Howland's coins would be real treasure today—worth as much as a quarter million dollars.

MANTOLOKING

In September, 1945, twelve year old Joseph Dowling of Philadelphia noticed the broken remains of an ancient chest half buried by sand at the edge of the surf on the beach at the quiet oceanside village of Mantoloking. Digging through the sand,

Joseph found a handful of gold coins, all English guineas from the late 1700s. Parents and friends aided in the search to find more gold coins in a treasure recovery that was kept relatively low-keyed. Four years later, treasure was again found on the same beach. This time, the word got out and the response was predictable.

Treasure Seekers
BOOTY FROM OLD WRECKS
FOUND ON JERSEY SHORE

MANTOLOKING, N.J.—This village of less than five hundred people has been the scene of frenzied doings in weeks past. Usually shore towns can look forward to an undisturbed rest after Labor Day. This year the Barnegat country is having a solid influx of visitors in the fall.

The drawing card, of course, is ancient treasure. The last week of September saw the discovery in the sands near here of a substantial number of eighteenth century coins plus some ancient articles of jewelry. One Philadelphia party claimed the recovery of ninety-three guinea and half-guinea pieces valued at $10 to $20 each. Some treasure trove must go unreported: it is safe to assume that the unpublicized winnings at least equal those that reach the press . . .

. . . Though every recovery is duly billed as "pirate treasure", the simple fact is that all recorded wrecks along the Jersey shore were prosaic traders, with the exception of a sprinkling of privateers and men-o'-war, none of the latter larger than a frigate.

The treasure hunter can, none the less, console himself with the fact that some of it must inevitably be recovered each year as the ocean yields up a bit of its claims in the autumn storms.

The initial discovery touching off this latest Jersey "gold rush" was made by a nine-year-old girl whose parents were preparing to close their beachfront house for the winter. Robert Nesmith, in his book *Dig for Pirate Treasure,* recorded the words of the girl, Gay Crampton, as she described her find in later years.

> It looked like a rock about three feet in diameter, composed of a hardened tar-like substance that had picked up small stones and sand . . . Fortunately the lump was not as heavy as stone and we gradually heaved it closer to the beach, where it was possible to break off small pieces.
>
> I ran to my mother with a piece and small round objects fell from it into her lap. She rubbed one in the sand and a gold coin appeared with the words "Georgius III Dei Gratia" faintly visible. It was dated 1789.

In other chunks were different sizes of shoe, hat, and belt buckles neatly packed together. Some dainty gold rings, cuff links . . .

The Mantoloking gold rush was sustained for nearly a month on reports of recoveries and news headlines. In the end, it appeared that some of the gold was not. Only the *Asbury Park Press* carried the factual update on October 20, 1949.

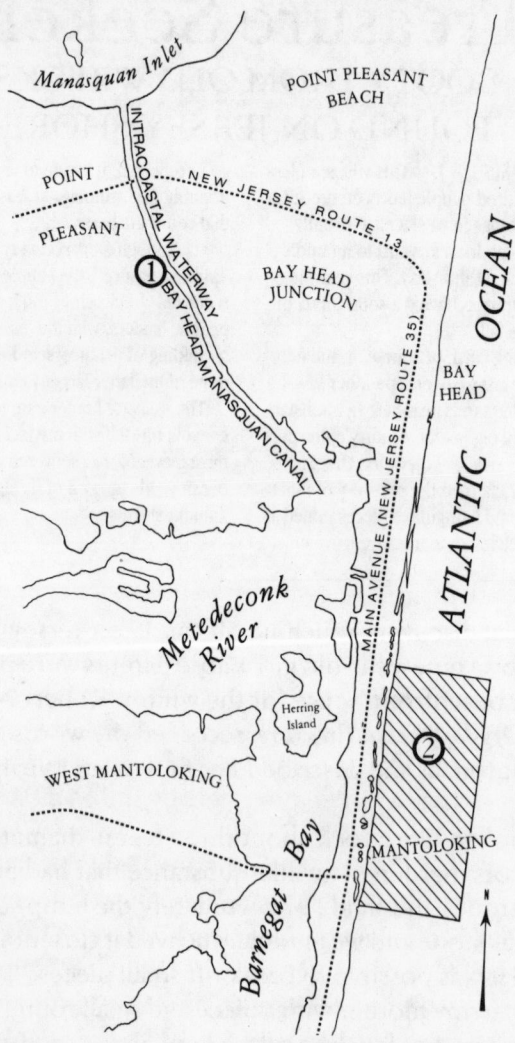

1. Site of the recovery of sixty-five United States gold coins in 1937.
2. The section of beach in Mantoloking where large recoveries were made in 1945 and 1949.

"Treasure" Labeled as Phony Gold

ALL IS NOT GOLD THAT GLITTERS

At least one of the treasure hunters who joined the rush of the 49ers (20th century style) to Mantoloking last week is disillusioned.

David Crampton, Montclair, a summer resident at the Shore community, suspected that the "gold" coins and jewelry found by his daughter, Gay, were as phony as a three dollar bill.

He was right. Tests disclosed that the "treasure" she picked up in the surf where a Philadelphia youth, Joseph Dowling, discovered a broken chest is all brass or pewter . . .

. . . (a curator of the Numismatic Society in New York) identified the coins, bearing the date 1789, as old time counterfeits made from dies similar to those used for British sovereigns.

Seems the theory is that when the Royal treasury got a little low, George III pulled a fast one on his country cousins in the colonies and pawned off a little brass cash. All apparently were of the type that unscrupulous ship captains used to foist off on the natives for trading purposes . . .

The coins were quality fakes and had apparently been hidden in resin or tar to elude customs inspections at the port of entry. Clever concealment was imperative, for in this era counterfeiting British coinage was high treason and a hanging offense. But, fake or not, the discovery touched off the Mantoloking gold rush in which the real thing was also found.

LONG BEACH ISLAND

Long Beach Island, an eighteen-mile-long barrier island, probably has the greatest concentration of wrecks on the Jersey shore, and it is not surprising that it also has one of the most productive mid-Atlantic coin beaches. Bounded on the north and south by two important colonial era inlets, the island was frequently visited by pirates and wartime privateers whose legends are exceeded in number only by the coins that wash up on the beaches.

Coins have been found the entire length of the island with the greatest concentration at Holgate, near the south end of the island, about two miles south of Beach Haven. The Holgate beach has yielded coins since the late 1800s, most Spanish silver pieces in two, four, and eight reale denominations and dating from 1720 to the early 1800s. Since 1732, the Spanish minted round coins and the eight reale piece, with the Pillars of Hercules on the reverse, became known as the pillar dollar. This coin was

the same size and actually the direct forerunner of the later
United States silver dollar. The number of coins recovered at
Holgate will never be known, but the total is certainly many
thousands. Prior to World War I, treasure hunters recovered
over 500 Spanish silver coins in a few days following a northeast storm.

Local treasure hunters find that walking the beach at the right
time is a simple, but effective, search method. Northeast storms
are usually followed by brisk west winds of high pressure weather
systems; after the storm has turned the beach over, the west wind
then blows the top layers of sand back into the sea. The coins
compact the sand beneath them, holding it in place as the adja-
cent loose sand blows away. Knowing this is the time to search,
experienced treasure hunters find the coins perched atop small
columns of sand.

Condition of the coins vary greatly; some have been reduced to
black silver sulfide through electro-chemical action of the seawater, others that were immersed near more chemically active
metals, such as iron, may appear in perfect condition. Some may
even have an attractive luster from the gentle polishing action of
the abrasive wet sand.

According to an enduring legend, an entire chest of Spanish
coins was recovered in the 1800s. The story has many versions
and dramatic alteration of the islands's configuration adds further
confusion. A century ago, Tucker's Island adjoined the south end
of Long Beach Island, and on it, in 1845, was built the Little Egg
Harbor Light. Later came a Life Saving Station, two hotels, a
school, and a number of houses. The sea built Tucker's Island,
and it also reclaimed it; the last buildings washed into the sea
in 1934 and today the island exists only in the memory of
the oldtimers.

The legend tells of two men anchoring a sloop off the beach at
Holgate and rowing ashore. At the Tucker's Island Life Saving
Station, the men inquired about local landmarks, especially about
the light and two large, old cedars. They slipped away in the
darkness and were next seen from the tower of the Station some
distance away, dragging an ironbound chest from a hole they had
dug between two prominent cedar trees. By the time the Station
crew reached the spot, the men had emptied the contents of the
chest into sacks and were rowing to their waiting sloop.

At the hole, the Life Saving Station crew found an empty chest,

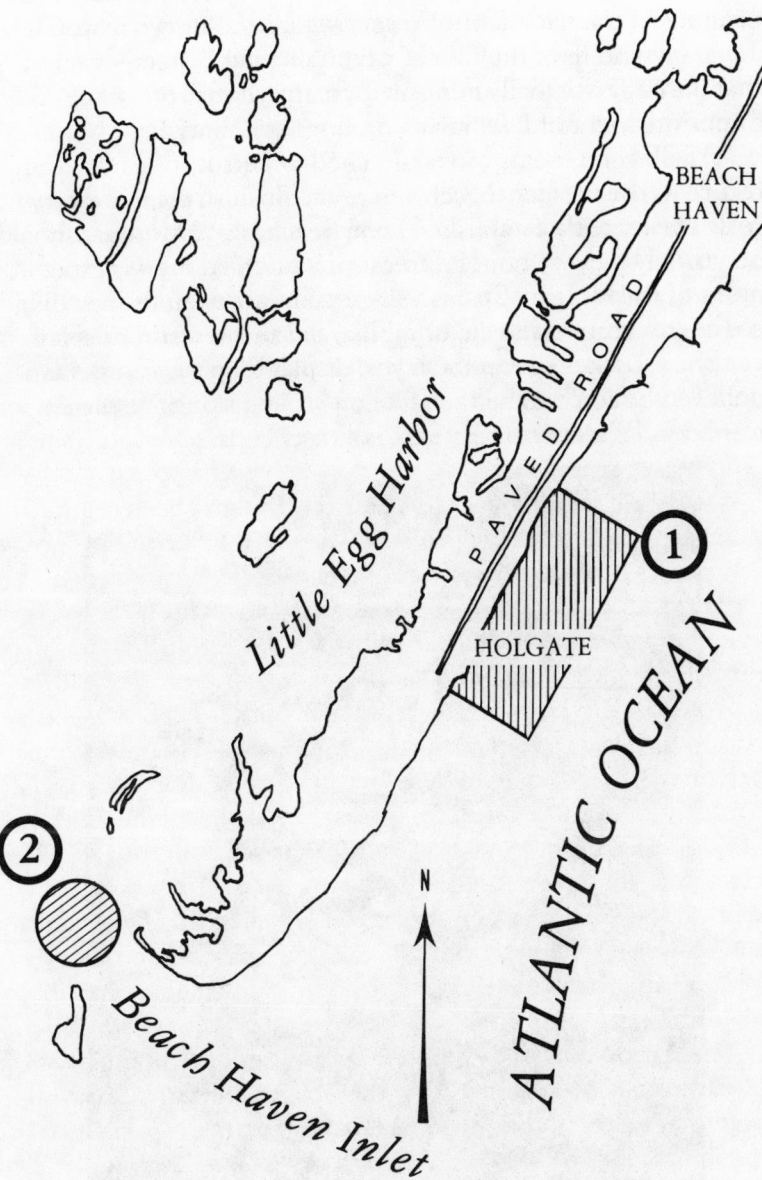

1. The section of beach in Holgate, at the south end of Long Beach Island, where Spanish silver coins have been recovered for over a century.
2. The approximate location of vanished Tucker's Island, probable site of the "Cutlass" treasure chest recovery. Dramatic alteration of coastal features in this area make the actual location uncertain.

a scattering of Spanish coins, a shovel, and a rusty cutlass. Some versions of the tale mention a yellowed, hand-drawn map. The legend would have the ring of a typical "pirate" story—except that the cutlass actually hung up for many years in the office of the Superintendent of Life Saving Stations at Asbury Park.

If the legend seems too far-fetched to pursue, one need only return to the Holgate beach where the Spanish coins are very real. The recently established Long Beach Island Museum should be visited by every hopeful treasure hunter. Along with specimens of the Holgate Spanish silver coins are exhibits including old charts, early island memorabilia, and an interesting display on vanished Tucker's Island. Oh yes, displayed in a glass case and believed by some to be the same one found alongside the empty ironbound chest a century ago, is a rusty cutlass . . .

Mr. Art Holzbauer, President of the Long Beach Island Historical Association, displaying the rusted cutlass believed to be the same one found at the legendary coin recovery site on Long Beach Island.

CHAPTER 9
The Silver Bars in the Arthur Kill

The most unlikely treasure ship ever to ply the waters of the mid-Atlantic or anywhere else was the *Harold*. Her lines would never inspire a model, and she had neither masts nor engines. She represented a family of craft that has served man well, yet enjoyed none of the respect and recognition given to other ships. None of her sisters ever aspired to fame, but the *Harold* earned a prominent place in the treasure lore of the coast, a remarkable achievement for a clumsy, square-ended barge.

On the evening of September 26, 1903, the *Harold* was taken in tow, her starboard side secured to the last in a string of thirteen smaller canal boats. Her cargo made the ungainly barge a true treasure ship, for stacked crosswise on her deck were 7,678 metal ingots, each two feet long and weighing one hundred pounds. The bars had been poured at a Mexican mine smelter and shipped by steamer to New York. At an East River dock, the shipment was loaded aboard the *Harold* for the thirty mile run to the American Smelting and Refining Company metal refinery at Perth Amboy, New Jersey. Each bar was composed of twenty-five percent lead and seventy-five percent silver. With four hundred tons of metal on her deck, the *Harold* was about to embark on a grander voyage than any galleon ever made, one bearing the awesome quantity of *three hundred tons* of silver.

As the sun set over New Jersey, the fourteen-boat tow, pulled by the Lehigh Valley Railroad tug *Ganoga,* made its way slowly past Governors Island and into Upper New York Bay, then along the Bayonne, New Jersey, docks before finally turning south into the Arthur Kill separating Staten Island and New Jersey. Aside from her top-heavy cargo, the *Harold* was otherwise empty and riding high out of the water, a little uncomfortably for her captain, Peter Moore. Moore became sleepy during the long hours beneath a nearly full moon and bedded down on the canal boat alongside.

All was serene as the *Ganoga* steadily towed the string toward Perth Amboy, and Moore slept contentedly. Suddenly, at 2:00 A.M. on the morning of the 27th, the *Harold* rolled heavily to starboard; almost all the bullion slid from the deck into the dark waters of the Kill. Freed of her burden, the barge quickly righted. When Moore awoke and collected his senses, he stared blankly at the empty deck, not noticing the few scattered bars that remained. Puzzled, he ran forward along the string and engaged in a brief shouted conversation with the captain of the *Ganoga,* all meaning of which was lost in the noisy distance that separated the tug from the first boat. Moore assumed that he had slept through a transfer; a smelter tug had come to speed the *Harold* to Perth Amboy, substituting an empty barge in her place. That seemed logical enough, and Moore went back to sleep.

At sunrise, the *Ganoga* nudged the *Harold* alongside the smelter dock. That the words of greeting have gone unrecorded is everyone's loss, especially Moore's answer to the question, "Where are the four hundred tons of bullion?" Moore and the tug captain were hustled aboard the first New York train to tell their stories amid suspicion that a brilliant highjacking might have taken place. Insurance interests and a salvage firm were notified quickly, with all aware that speed and secrecy were of the utmost importance. The Arthur Kill was a rich shellfish ground and oystermen worked the beds daily, probing and raking the bottom. Industrial piracy was another problem, for harbor barges were plundered regularly. What any oysterman or harbor pirate would do if they knew of the loss chilled the insurance underwriters.

It was deduced that the bullion was lost somewhere in the twelve miles of the Arthur Kill. Neither Moore nor the tug captain had taken bearings during their confused conversation the previous night, but recollection of the moon's position helped establish the approximate location as the southern part of the Kill. The salvage was assigned to Captain William H. Timmans of the Baxter Wrecking Company who, with a trusted crew, began "fishing" from a steam launch before nightfall.

With the assumption that the *Harold* had touched bottom to cause the loss, the first areas searched were the points of mud that

protrude into the channel. When that failed, a broad bottom
survey with sounding weights was begun. Day after day, Timmans searched only when no other boats were near and also well
beyond the estimated site of the loss so as not to attract attention
to any one area. After a week of futile effort, many wondered if
highjacking weren't the answer after all.

Finally, on October 5th, off Sewaren, New Jersey, the sounding weights struck metal repeatedly and two salvage vessels were
called in. A clambucket was dropped to the bottom and retrieved
with a ton of mud and fifteen of the lost silver bars. The operation
continued for a week, then divers were sent down to pick up any
remaining visible bars. By October 16th, over 6,000 ingots had
been recovered and delivered to the smelter dock.

In 1903, the price of both silver and lead were severely
depressed because of politics and overproduction from the
western mines; fine silver was worth only fifty cents per Troy
ounce and lead about three cents per pound. Since the *Harold*'s
bullion cargo required further refining, its actual value was about
half that. Newspapers reported the value of the lost cargo to be
only a little over $100,000.

On October 17th, the cloak of secrecy was lifted and the *New
York Times* belatedly reported the loss and subsequent salvage of
most of the bullion. The article concluded with the words of
Captain Baxter, manager of the salvage company.

"They have the worst pirates along
the coast down that way", he said.
"They'll think nothing of shooting a
barge captain. If they had known all
that bullion was there, they would
have got it somehow. We fairly out-
witted them this time. It was one of
the most peculiar cases we've ever
had. Those men on the tow were the
dumbest skunks I've ever had to do
with."

. . . Captain Baxter added that the
next few days would decide how
long he would keep the divers hunting for further salvage, but he was
satisfied that there was not enough
left on the bottom to make it worth
any amateur wrecker's while to turn
in and help without an invitation.

Captain Baxter may have been right about the approximately 1,400 silver-lead bars left in the mud of the Arthur Kill—in 1903. Today, however, silver is worth far more than fifty cents per ounce, and in the remaining lost ingots are 1,260,000 Troy ounces of silver worth about $17,000,000. That many zeros refresh the memory and, after seventy-seven long years, the *New York Times* had occasion to print a follow-up on December 12, 1980.

> ## *Mystery Boat with Diving Gear Plies Arthur Kill Where Silver Cargo Was Lost in '03*

The article told of renewed interest among salvors. The "mystery boat" proved merely the tip of the iceberg for, by spring of 1981, at least three groups publicly announced they would attempt to salvage the silver treasure. The competition quickly put everything into the hands of attorneys and courts. The British

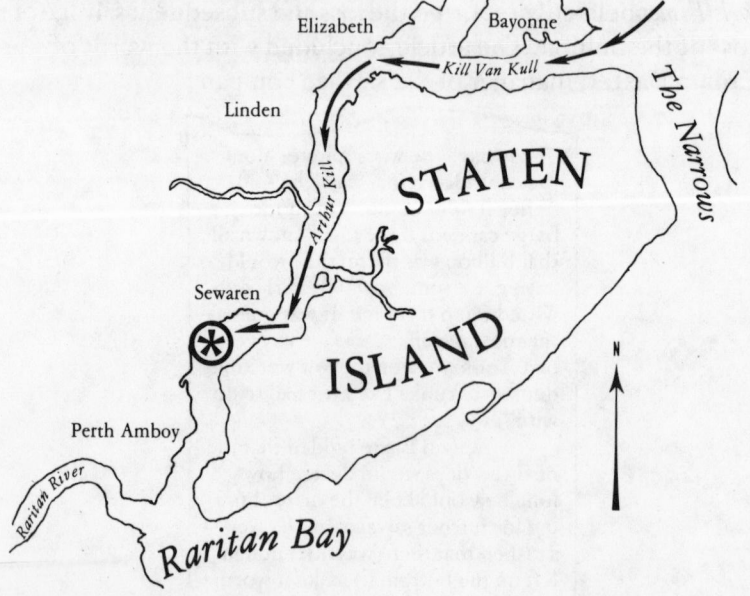

New York Harbor and the Arthur Kill. The route of the *Ganoga* tow is indicated. At a point in the Kill off Sewaren, NJ, the silver cargo was dumped. Today's primary search areas are indicated.

and Foreign Insurance Company ownership claim is still effective today, and the company announced signing an agreement with one salvage group in 1980 on the basis of a three-to-one salvor-company division. All interests are now mired in a complex legal battle to claim right of "first salvor" and thus legal authority to commence salvage.

There has already been sabotage of equipment, a gun brandishing incident, and United States Coast Guard involvement. One group claims to have salvaged one of the silver-lead bars, then returned it to the deep marked with a buoy which mysteriously disappeared. That single bar, incidentally, was worth nearly $10,000.

When a Federal District Court does grant someone salvage rights, they will be able to employ state-of-the-art technology to locate the treasure. Captain Timmans' sounding weights have been replaced by sub-bottom profilers, electronic instrumentation that can literally "see" into the silt and mud covering the silver. Actual salvage will require an industrial dredging operation conducted at considerable expense, but one easily afforded considering the potential value of the recovery. The next major mid-Atlantic treasure recovery may well be the millions of dollars of silver at the bottom of the Arthur Kill.

The bars lie covered by many feet of oily silt beneath the polluted water of one of the most developed and busiest waterways in the nation. There are no palm trees, coral reefs, or pieces of eight here, but with $17,000,000 in silver at stake, few treasure salvors object to the lack of romance.

PART III

New York Treasures

CHAPTER 10
The New York Coast

The coast of New York is composed of two contrasting parts; the maze of inland waterways and bays of the nation's greatest harbor, and 120 miles of barrier islands and beach on Long Island. The general east-west alignment of Long Island made it a lesser navigation hazard than New Jersey, for ships in northeast winds could more easily maintain their offshore sailing distance. However, shipping traffic was heavy and Long Island claimed over one thousand wrecks, a toll that prompted the establishment of thirty Life Saving Stations, a concentration second only to New Jersey. Long Island's first lighthouse was built at Montauk Point, the eastern extremity of the island, in 1797. The Fire Island Light was first lit in 1825, then rebuilt in 1858 as a greatly improved 170-foot tower, the same year the Shinnecock light at Ponquogue Point was put into service. Competition among Long Island's wreckers was particularly fierce, and the dominant were the most ruthless. The most notorious reputations went to the Fire Island wreckers, who fully lived up to their billing as "land pirates."

Pirates of the seagoing variety abounded on eastern Long Island, both in legend and fact. Many historians, even those usually disdaining "pirate" tales, believe that the well-traveled Captain William Kidd buried much of his loot on Gardiner's Island, about ten miles west of Montauk. A great deal of pick and shovel work has gone into the search there, but Kidd and his crew, as history has proven, were expert at hiding treasure.

Another of the many pirates to visit Long Island was the infamous Charles Gibbs. Gibbs operated in the 1820s, the last years for piracy, and his final crime was commandeering a brig by murdering her captain. Off Long Island, Gibbs loaded four sacks, containing 5,000 pillar dollars each, into small boats, then scuttled the brig. Some of the silver was lost in the surf, but Gibbs is purported to have buried the rest on "Barron Island"—which might be a place name or a description—not far from Southampton, then fled. Weeks later, he was caught, tried, and sentenced to death. The burial of the silver was revealed in testimony during his trial and is contained in records of the United States Court of the Southern District of New York. Gibbs never returned to the treasure. He was hanged in 1831.

The frequency of wrecks on Long Island declined significantly when the lightship system was established about the turn of the century. Trans-Atlantic shipping now steered for the Nantucket Lightship sixty miles east of Montauk, rather than attempting to pick up land beacons near the rocks and shoals. From Nantucket Lightship, course was then set for Ambrose Lightship at the seaward approach to New York harbor.

Unlike the long, desolate beaches of Long Island, New York harbor has seen continuous heavy activity for 350 years. Collectively, all the bays, sounds, and rivers of the harbor have over one hundred miles of navigable waterways, the bottoms of which are paved with wrecks and debris from hundreds of ships and smaller craft that have been abandoned or lost through fire, collisions, and other accidents. One of the harbor's most famous treasures is one which has been salvaged, although several treasure salvage books continue to list it. On March 10, 1928, the Italian liner *Roma* was loading a consignment of $3,000,000 in gold specie and bullion at the foot of West Fifty-Seventh Street. The gold was packed in sixty small kegs, each the size of a one gallon container and weighing 225 pounds, and worth $50,000 each. As the last of it was hoisted, the net sling broke and dumped two kegs into the Hudson. Newspaper headlines of lost gold immediately attracted crowds to the waterfront to watch divers attempt the salvage. For two days, the hunt proved futile, and as crowds drifted away the belief grew that the gold remained in the riverbottom mud. In the 1950's, SCUBA divers were seen on several occasions prowling the dark waters under Pier 97 seeking the treasure. They evidently did not know that three days after it was lost, divers recovered the first keg in forty feet of water and six feet of black ooze. The second keg was recovered with a clamshell from fourteen feet of ooze.

While the *Roma*'s treasure was not lost at all, many others in New York, both in the harbor and on the beaches of Long Island, still await recovery.

CHAPTER 11

The Wreck of the
H.M.S. Hussar

The summer of 1780 found the war going badly for Britain.
Morale was low; many British and Hessian troops had gone
unpaid for a year while enduring a worrisome persistence from
the ragtag Continental Army. Washington had reversed many of
his early defeats and now held key positions surrounding New
York. The British command was already making plans for the
inevitable evacuation of the city and port.

Sailing into this wartime drama came the H.M.S. *Hussar,* a new
twenty-eight gun frigate bearing a most welcome shipment from
London, a large military payroll of gold, silver, and copper coins
worth nearly two million pounds. The *Hussar* anchored in New
York Harbor on September 13, 1780. After that, events become
shrouded in the veil of wartime secrecy and confusion stemming
from the imminent evacuation. The *Hussar* quickly received
orders to clear port and proceed to New England, taking a route
up the East River, through Hell Gate, and into Long Island Sound.
Many observers, including a number of American spies, were
convinced the ship still had aboard much of the British payroll.

The passage through aptly named Hell Gate remains today one
of the more dangerous in the United States. It is a crooked,
rock-lined channel through which, at tidal changes, surge enormous volumes of water in swift, unpredictable currents. Mariners
are still uneasy about Hell Gate, even after millions have been
spent blasting rock to clear and straighten the channel. During
the colonial days it was far worse; military records show that one
out of every twenty-five ships that attempted the passage were
seriously damaged or sunk.

The unfortunate *Hussar* became one of those statistics. Caught in a tidal surge, the frigate struck and holed on Pot Rock, an obstruction long since removed, then struggled clear of the Gate before sinking a short distance off what is now 132nd Street in the Bronx. Under the watchful eyes of American spies, the British attempted a hurried salvage, the first of many efforts to come, while her masts were still above water. The odds were against the British, for the currents, poor visibility, limited salvage technology, and the brief time remaining before the evacuation all stood in the way of success.

Silt began burying the wreck immediately, but the *Hussar* and her reputed treasure were hardly forgotten. Interest was revived again during the War of 1812, when the British unexpectedly announced that the *Hussar* had not carried any treasure when she sank three decades earlier. Many thought the announcement a wartime ploy to discourage American salvage attempts, assuming that if Britain won the war, the Admiralty itself would salvage the *Hussar.* The next major attempt was made in 1818, but only an anchor and several cannon were raised. In 1820, a diving bell was employed and entry made into the hull. A brass plaque and other artifacts were recovered that are now reportedly in possession of Columbia University. Diving bells were tried again in 1848 by a well-financed British expedition but the clumsy bells proved impractical in the Hell Gate currents. Another group even secured cables to the stern of the sunken frigate but were unable to move it. As late as 1852, the wreck was still buoyed as a hazard to navigation.

The last decades of the nineteenth century saw several attempts, involving stock-funded companies operating under questionable government contracts. The United States Treasury claimed a portion of the treasure, citing the fact that the *Hussar,* an enemy ship, sank in wartime. No one had yet proven positively that there actually was treasure aboard the *Hussar,* but the Treasury Department's claim was proof enough for many hopeful salvors.

The *Hussar* and her unproven golden fortune had rested on the bottom for 150 years, but they became front page news again when Simon Lake, a marine inventor, tried his luck in the 1930s. Lake thought success could be achieved through use of a small submarine, allowing divers to work the bottom while anchored against the current. The 1930s were very busy years for mid-Atlantic treasure salvors, for as Lake prepared for his attempt on the *Hussar,* other operations were proceeding simultaneously on the *Merida* off Virginia and the *deBraak* in Delaware. The *New York Times* still found room to report on Lake's quest on August 6, 1935.

HUSSAR GOLD QUEST RESUMED BY INVENTOR

Simon Lake In "Baby" Submarine To Investigate

Simon Lake's quest for the half legendary gold of the British ship Hussar, which sank in 1780 in the East River off what is now 132nd Street, was resumed again yesterday in the swift rip tides and currents of the Hell Gate vicinity.

Mr. Lake, the submarine inventor, has been working intermittantly for months, adapting and perfecting his diving apparatus of a "baby" submarine and hinged steel tube to the difficult conditions encountered in the East River. He stopped work some time ago, after finding three hulks at different spots in

the vicinity of where the Hussar sank, all three of them covered with about fifteen feet of silt. In the interval, Mr. Lake installed a glass window in the bottom of the bow of the submarine. The craft is serviced from a long tube from a surface vessel. He also made a probing device which can be operated outside the submarine, but controlled by those within it . . .

The Hussar, according to a report that has never been fully substantiated, carried treasure variously estimated at $4,000,000 to $5,000,000 when she sank.

Simon Lake and his crews worked through the summer and fall of 1935, then resumed operations in June, 1936. On September 26, Lake issued a very encouraging statement.

LAKE THINKS HULK IS TREASURE SHIP

INVENTOR THINKS HE HAS FOUND WRECK OF FRIGATE HUSSAR IN EAST RIVER

Carried $1,800,000 in Gold

PROBING REVEALED HARD TIMBERS INDICATED POSITION, AND TREASURY IS NOTIFIED

Simon Lake, veteran submarine enthusiast, has notified the Treasury Department at Washington that he has discovered a hulk in the East River which he believes to be the

almost fabulous vessel H.M.S. Hussar, a British frigate which sank in 1780 with, possibly, $1,800,000 in gold aboard.

Summoning reporters to his room at 108

West Forty-Third Street yesterday afternoon, the inventor declared, "If I were a betting man, I would lay 100 to 1 that the Hussar has been found at last. For fifty years I have been speculating on the likelihood of locating this ship and within six weeks I expect to step within her hold. Now, nobody can tell me what gold there is. It is not gold so much as the satisfaction of solving the riddle, though some gold would do no harm."

On September 4, his seventieth birthday, Mr. Lake struck the Hussar, he contends. Sounding operations were being conducted by him about fifty yards offshore between East 130th and East 140th Streets, the Bronx, on the East River.

Here, in the shadow of the busy College Point Ferry Terminus, his eighty foot beam was plunging into the murky water and through two fathoms of soft silt.

"All on board recognized the tell-tale sound of wood when the beam landed", Mr. Lake said, "and we more or less expected to find a spongy, water-logged raft, but instead the screw revealed hardwood, possibly teak, and we felt that we had found the Hussar.

"Previous salvage attempts had established her position as just over a ledge, with her bow in fifty feet of water and her stern twenty feet lower", he continued.

"I find such a ledge extends nearly a mile along the shore and drops down in some places to the depth mentioned. I think the hulk I located lies in a position corresponding to that of the Hussar.

"It is covered with twelve feet of silt which must be pumped off before I send a submarine down to settle on the frigate's decks. From that point, divers can step into the hold with jets and suction pumps to see whether the treasure is fact or fable.

"My probing leads me to believe that the Hussar could very well be raised for exhibition at the World's Fair. I hope to begin work under supervision of the Coast Guard within one month."

For several weeks following the announcement, large crowds gathered on the Bronx shore to watch the progress of the operation, but gradually lost interest as, day after day, Lake's divers came to the surface without treasure. Simon Lake, plagued by funding and legal problems, finally abandoned his four year attempt in 1937.

Nothing more was heard of the *Hussar* until 1967 when unsubstantiated reports told of some success. It seems a barge anchored near the site and began taking great clambucket bites out of the riverbottom. Rumors spread that several hundred gold guineas, the type of coins that would have been part of the British payroll aboard the *Hussar,* had been recovered. The operations continued for several weeks but found only bits of wood and rusted iron objects.

Today, the *Hussar* lies covered by more silt and mud than ever and may even be partly under an encroaching landfill working its way out from the Bronx shore. Whether the gold fortune is there still remains to be proven, but today's price of gold will doubtlessly inspire other attempts.

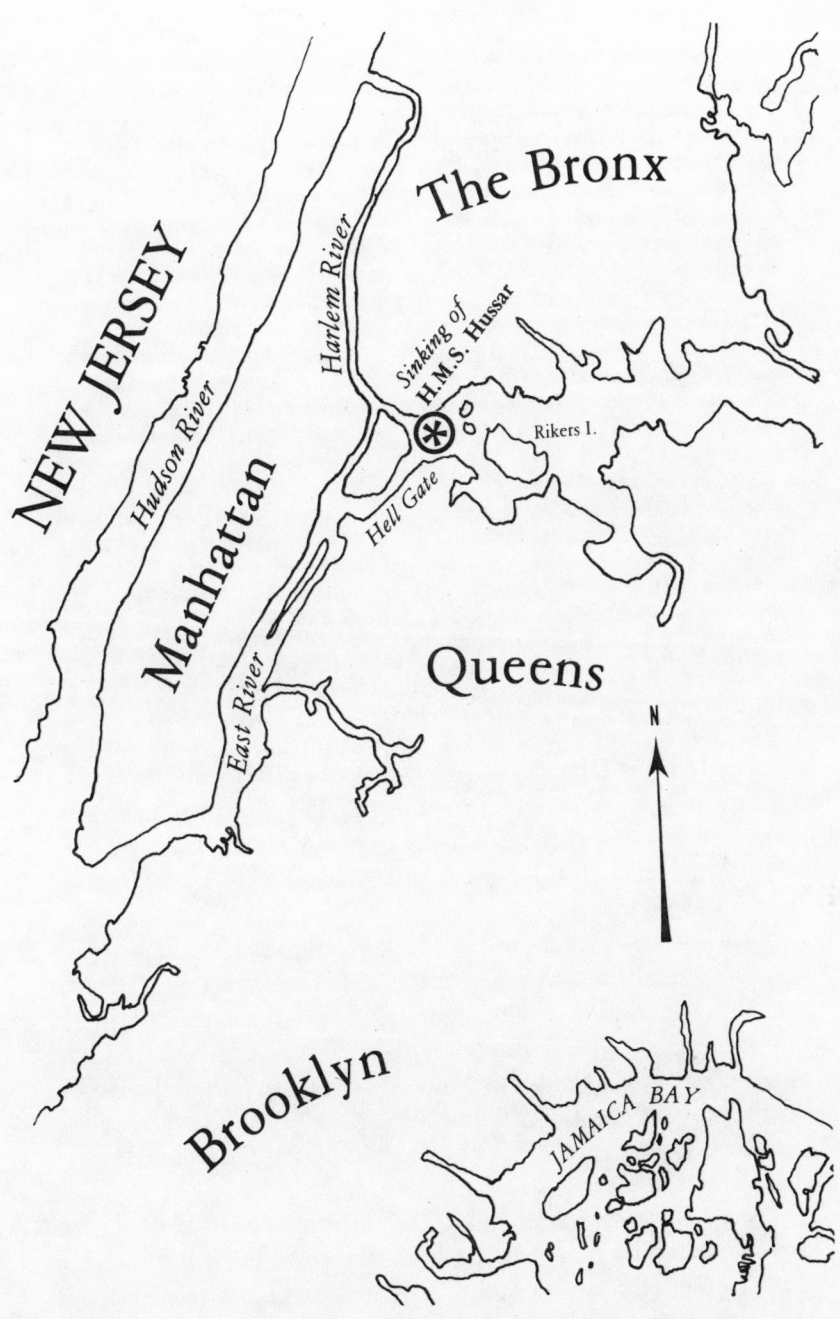

New York Harbor, showing the site of the sinking of the H.M.S. *Hussar* off 135th Street in the South Bronx.

CHAPTER 12

The Long Island "Money Wreck" and Coin Beach

The "Money Wreck" of Long Island is one of those treasure stories that seems to tread the thin line between fact and legend; if color and circumstance were the sole determining points, the story might be discounted as legend. But confirmation has come in a most convincing fashion—as the many Spanish silver coins that have washed up on the Hampton beaches. The story has many versions, but most all agree on the main points.

In November, 1816, a strange sail appeared off the barrier beaches near Southampton, and old Hampton seamen noted her to be of similar rig to the East African slavers they had seen earlier during their seafaring years. They watched as the ship sailed steadily on an unusual tack, and some even guessed her wheel was lashed down. Time proved them correct, for several days later the ship was seen again, ten miles to the west and grounded on a bar opposite Shinnecock Bay. Upon grounding, the ship had snapped a mast and settled with a heavy list onto the shoal. The following day, three men rowed out to the derelict to find a mystery rivaling that of the celebrated *Marie Celeste.* The vessel was found completely abandoned; it had no name plate, no papers or records, yet a full store of supplies and an armory of pistols, cutlasses, and muskets. Abandonment seemed to have been made in great haste not many days before.

The local Wreckmaster took charge of the grounded ship, arranged a public auction, sold the stores, and disposed of the hull to a team of local wreckers who had formed a company for the purpose of breaking it up for planks and timbers. It was during the auction that the first of the coins were found that would make the wreck a treasure ship. They were Spanish pillar dollars, the popular one-ounce silver coin commonly circulated in the United States. The first was found lodged in a deadeye in the rigging. That discovery was attributed to chance and aroused no great interest, but when a second coin was found on the beach opposite the wreck, some of the locals began to wonder.

One of the curious was Henry Green, a young Southampton whaler just back from a voyage. Green, together with another local whaler, Franklin Jagger, had finished hunting ducks on the deserted beach near the wreck. It was late afternoon when they laid their guns aside, yielded to their curiosity, and went aboard the wreck. Rummaging about the hulk, they found another pillar dollar on the floor of the cabin. They left the wreck at last light, but the discovery of the coin had piqued their interest. They returned again at low tide the following night, this time with a tin lantern to conduct a more thorough search. After several hours of searching the stripped hulk, they were about to leave when they noticed a split seam in the sagging overhead paneling of the cabin ceiling. Prying down a section of the ceiling, they were simultaneously startled and rewarded by a cascade of hundreds of silver coins. As the coins fell, Jagger dropped the lantern, plunging the cabin into darkness. On their hands and knees, Green and Jagger groped about the dark cabin floor gathering all the coins they could find and carry, then left. For several nights following, the two whalers secretly boarded the shoaled hulk seeking more Spanish silver.

It was already December and the northeast storms were upon the coast. The wrecking company that purchased the hulk never had the chance to break it up, for the sea beat them to it. One heavy storm did the job, littering the beaches for miles with the wreckage of the nameless ship. Some years after the ship broke up, quantities of Spanish silver coins began appearing on the Shinnecock beaches. All were dated between 1740 and 1790, all were pillar dollars, and they were found in quantities that made searches profitable. After severe northeast storms, local farmers sometimes led their teams to the beaches to plow up the sand; one farmer reportedly found sixty pillar dollars in a single day.

An apparent answer to the mystery of the abandoned wreck and its vanished crew was established by connecting it with an incident that took place on the Easthampton beaches and became known later. Three days before the derelict grounded at Shinnecock, a similar vessel anchored off the Easthampton bar. A small crew rowed ashore in two yawls, both bearing many bags of silver coins for burial, but a group of Long Island's notorious wreckers, having received word of what would take place, was waiting for them. The crew was murdered, but scuttling the ship proved more difficult. In order to remove the evidence from their section of beach, they lashed the wheel in place, gave the ship some sail, and sent it off on a tack along the coast.

These events have been recorded in old issues of the *Long Island Forum*, and all accounts indicate they took place in the year 1816. The story is similar to the adventures of the pirate Charles Gibbs in the same area in 1830. Whether there is a tie between the stories, or whether they might even be the same, is not clear. Whatever the true story, the existence of the coins is not questioned. As late as 1959, the *Long Island Forum* reported that Spanish pillar dollars were still being found on the beaches from Shinnecock to Easthampton. It would be interesting to find the exact location where the "Money Ship" broke up, perhaps even locate the keel of the wreck, if it is still there. The sands there might hold thousands of Spanish pillar dollars, a treasure from the days one hundred and sixty years ago when eastern Long Island was the domain of pirates and wreckers.

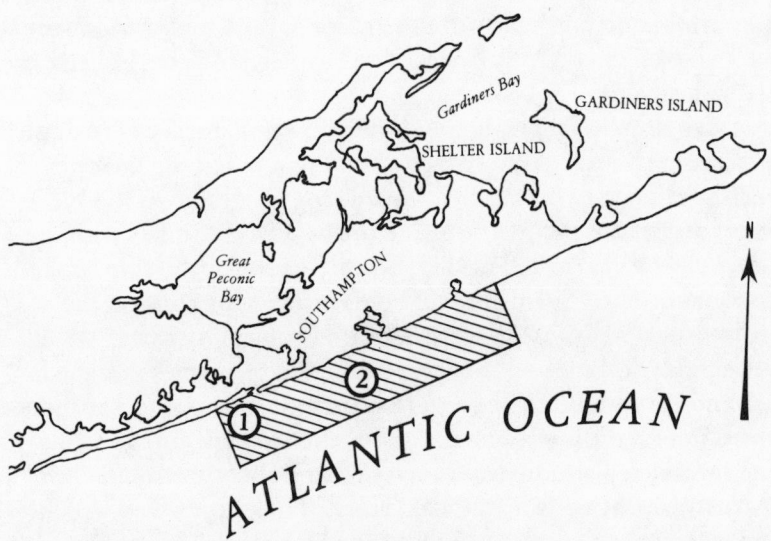

Eastern Long Island
1. Approximate site of the "Money Ship" wreck.
2. The long section of Long Island beach where Spanish silver pillar dollars have been recovered.

CHAPTER 13
"CQD . . . Save the Republic"

In the early 1900's, Guglielmo Marconi's wireless telegraph was an enormous advance to maritime safety. For the first time, ships unseen could communicate with each other as well as with distant land stations. The potential of wireless for aiding distressed ships was obvious, but the system had yet to be proved in an actual major emergency. In 1909, the Marconi wireless system was still in its infancy; only 180 ships in the world were rigged with the new apparatus. One was the three-year-old White Star liner *Republic*, over 500 feet long, displacing 15,000 tons, and one of the fastest liners in trans-Atlantic service. In the early morning hours of January 23, 1909, the *Republic* was at sea, outbound from New York for the Mediterranean.

The *Republic* was not alone as she crept at half speed through a dense Atlantic fog preceded by throaty blasts of her foghorn. She was twenty miles south of the Nantucket Lightship and some sixty miles due east of Montauk Point, Long Island, in one of the busiest shipping lanes in the world. Virtually all trans-Atlantic traffic, inbound and outbound, good weather and bad, passed just south of the lightship. At this particular moment in history, one of the inbound ships was the 8,000-ton displacement *Florida*, a steamer of the Lloyd Italiano Line, nearing completion of her voyage from Naples to New York.

Marconi land station operators in Massachusetts, Rhode Island, and Long Island were handling the routine flow of messages to, from, and between ships, clearing and directing communications on the common frequency. At 5:30 A.M., Marconi operators at several land stations picked up a signal breaking in over the authorized traffic.

CQ CQ CQ CQ CQ
A repetitive "CQ" was the code informing all ship and land

wireless operators to cease sending immediately, thus clearing the frequency for a signal of unusual importance. All over the coast, the clacking Morse keys went silent as operators waited with full attention. Without the usual background sending interference, the signal resumed clear and unmistakable.

CQD KC CQD KC CQD KC

The addition of the code letter "D" meant danger; the combination code sequence "CQD", coming from the dense Atlantic fog somewhere east of Long Island, was a general call for immediate assistance and was authorized for use only in the most extreme emergency at sea. "KC," as every Marconi operator knew, was the identification code for the mighty White Star liner *Republic*. The land operators relayed the signal from their powerful transmitters, acknowledging receipt of the "CQD" and bringing to a halt all wireless traffic for 500 miles. Then, after brief silence, the Morse keys clacked again on impulse from the lone signal coming out of the Atlantic fog.

CQD KC RAMMED BY UNKNOWN SHIP 26 MILES SOUTH OF NANTUCKET LATITUDE 40.17 LONGITUDE 70 CQD KC

The signal was received by eight land stations and wireless equipped ships; the land station operators began relaying and coordinating assistance messages, while the captains of five ships steered for Nantucket, running through the fog at full steam.

There had been no witnesses to the collision when the *Florida* struck the *Republic* amidships, cutting a huge hole deep into the engine room of the larger liner, through which icy seawater poured in torrents. After the collision, the *Florida,* not rigged with wireless, her bow stove in and taking water, staggered back into the fog. The two severely damaged ships were alone on the fogbound sea, their sole hope for assistance riding on the clacking Morse key in the wireless room of the listing *Republic*. The drama that followed would take over a day, with every step told over the wireless. From land stations, the call went out to other ships:

TO REVENUE CUTTER GRESHAM, BOSTON: STEAMER REPUBLIC IN DISTRESS AND SINKING, LATITUDE 40.17 LONGITUDE 70

From White Star Line offices in New York to U.S. Navy Destroyer *Seneca:*

REPUBLIC AND FLORIDA ARE DRIFTING SOMEWHERE NEAR NANTUCKET SHOALS LIGHT.

DO ALL YOU CAN TO SAVE THE REPUBLIC.
From the White Star Line steamer *Baltic* to New York:
RECEIVED MESSAGE FROM REPUBLIC OF RAMMING.
WILL PROCEED TO HER ASSISTANCE. REACH HER AT
11:00. NOW 115 EAST OF AMBROSE.
From the *Republic:*
REPUBLIC CAN REMAIN AFLOAT TWO HOURS
LONGER. ALL PASSENGERS AND THREE QUARTERS OF
CREW TRANSFERRED TO FLORIDA. OTHERS
PREPARING TO LEAVE THE SHIP.
From the *Baltic:*
BALTIC FOUND FLORIDA AND REPUBLIC AND IS
NOW STANDING BY TO RENDER ASSISTANCE.
From the *Seneca:*
ALL HANDS OFF. REPUBLIC SINKING FAST. CAPT.
SEALBY, IN BOAT ALONGSIDE, REFUSED TO LEAVE
HER UNTIL OUT OF SIGHT.

Thirty-nine hours after the collision, the *Republic* lifted her bow into the fog, then slid beneath the Atlantic. The fog had never lifted, an east wind was picking up, and weather conditions were deteriorating. Before a northeast storm swept the sea, 1,650 people were brought safely to New York. The Marconi wireless had averted a catastrophe.

The S.S *Republic,* sunk in collision with the S.S. *Florida* about sixty miles east of Montauk Point, Long Island. The *Republic* sank with $3,000,000 in U.S. gold eagles and is now the target of treasure salvors. Courtesy Mariners' Museum, Newport News, VA.

When the *Republic* sank, she was under a slow, one knot tow in a futile race against time to reach the Nantucket shoals where salvage would have been possible. Her grave is in forty fathoms of water, nine miles south by east from the Nantucket Lightship and about seventy miles due east of Montauk Point. In 1909, the wreck was too deep for salvage, so the *Republic* became only a memory. But it was one that would endure, for her cargo included $3,000,000 in gold.

Forty-seven years later, another great maritime tragedy, one strikingly similar, would occur in almost the exact same spot. In an age of electronics and radar, in an accident that was inexcusable, the *Stockholm* rammed the *Andrea Doria,* sending the latter to join the rusted hulk of the *Republic* on the bottom. Today, SCUBA divers make almost routine visits to the *Andrea Doria* in 190 feet of water, and the equipment now exists to make salvage a possibility.

If the *Andrea Doria* can be reached, so can the *Republic,* along with her cargo of gold which is now worth an enormous sum. Treasure salvors, among them New Jersey diver Russ Langella, already have their eye on the *Republic,*as reported in a July 26, 1981, article in the *Newark Star-Ledger.*

. . . Langella sees a big future in salvage work. He's particularly interested in the Republic, which sank in 1909, just a few miles from the spot where the Andrea Doria went down in 1956. The Republic is widely believed to have been carrying $3 million dollars worth of $10 U.S. gold pieces called eagles. Langella claims to have confirmed this story.

"That's $3 million then", Langella says. "It would be about $115 million today. And it's funny. There are several people who have had the approximate location of the wreck. You talk to people and they'll say, 'Oh, yeah, I fish on it'. And we have made some dives, and we have come up with some evidence that this really is the Republic.

"But try to prove that the ship really had that gold on it, had money on it. It took us three years with one guy working, to finally come up with the proof we needed. Three years. Because you always hear, 'Hey, this wreck is over here, it's got $10 million on it. And this one over here has $5 million.'

"But then start tracking these things down, and doing some research on a ship, and you'll find it's nothing. It's all hearsay in other words. Someone wrote a story forty years ago, and just heard rumors at the time that the ship had gold on it, but went ahead and wrote it, and all of a sudden, that little story, which was really hearsay, is now considered hard fact."

Langella's words and attitude, as well as his recognition of the importance of research, reflects cold, hard realism, not glowing romanticism, and is a mark of the modern, professional salvor. But the gold of the *Republic* is not just there for the taking. The wreck lies at the extreme working limit of compressed air SCUBA and the dangers are many; the location is known for bad weather, cold water, and a profusion of sharks. The wreck itself is largely collapsed, and penetration of the hull or superstructure would be difficult and dangerous. It is hardly a job for the weekend diver.

But, if $115,000,000 in gold is there, as Langella believes, someone will attempt the salvage. Today's technology provides the means, and that much gold provides the incentive.

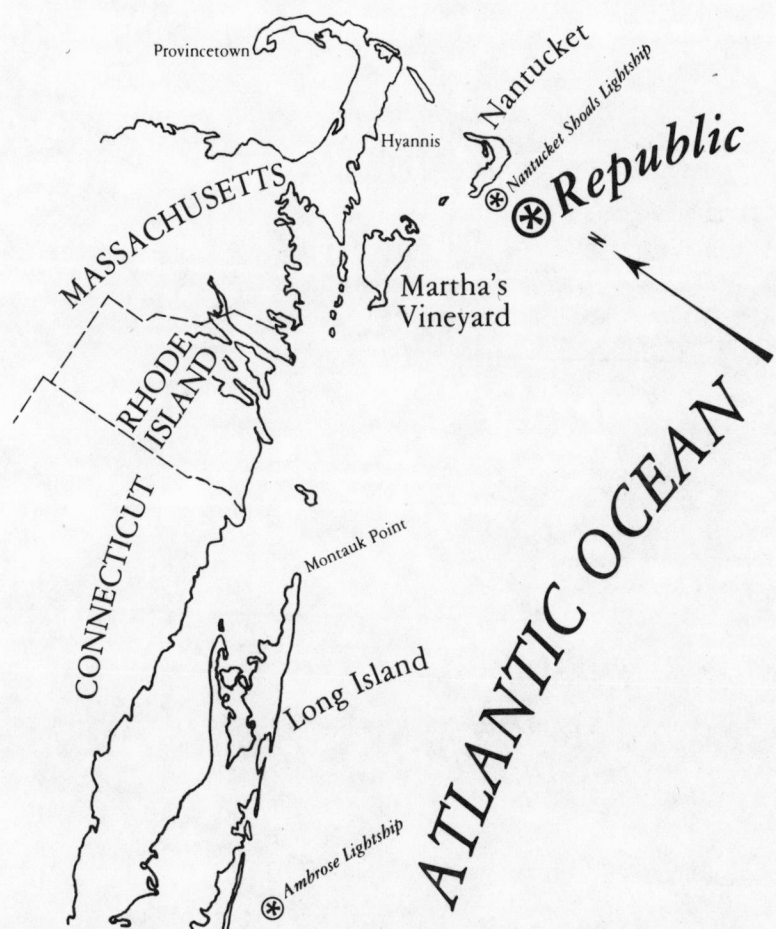

Location of the wrecksite of the *Republic* in forty fathoms of water about nine miles south by east from the Nantucket Lightship.

PART IV

Delaware Treasures

CHAPTER 14
The Delaware Coast

Delaware's coast fronting directly on the Atlantic is only twenty-five miles long, all of it barrier beach and broken only by the Indian River Inlet. Another fifty miles of waterfront faces the broad reaches of Delaware Bay. Despite its diminutive geographic size, Delaware has claimed over two hundred early shipwrecks and had two Life Saving Stations erected on its Atlantic coast.

Safe passage into Delaware Bay was always dependent upon safely navigating past Cape Henlopen, a low sand spit that divides the Bay from the open sea and juts precariously near the main shipping channel leading to the busy Philadelphia area ports. One of the nation's first lighthouses was constructed there in 1767. The Cape Henlopen light served as a beacon for well over a century and survived wartime burnings and constant beach erosion before falling victim to a northeast storm in 1926 when the historic stone tower collapsed into the sea.

The southern limit of Delaware's Atlantic coastline is the Maryland border. The Fenwick Island lighthouse was put into service here in 1859 to mark the treacherous offshore Fenwick Shoals. The light remains in operation today.

Nearly all of Delaware's Atlantic coast has been protected from commercial development through establishment of two State Parks, Cape Henlopen in the north and Delaware Seashore along the barrier beaches to the south. The little town of Lewes, near Cape Henlopen, is one of the more interesting historic sites along the mid-Atlantic coast. Originally founded as a Dutch settlement 350 years ago, Lewes has maintained its quaint, distinctive atmosphere reflecting a rich maritime heritage.

Delaware's coastal lore includes many pirate legends, most centering about the bay waterfront near Blackbird Creek, Milford, and Bombay Hook. Elaborately stamped silver bars, popularly believed to be pirate loot, were recovered in these areas. The most noted of the pirates to operate in Delaware Bay was Edward Teach who, with many contemporaries, frequently visited both the New Jersey and Delaware shores.

Even though its Atlantic coast is small, Delaware claims the most legendary and sought after of all mid-Atlantic treasure shipwrecks, as well as a coin beach that is the most productive of any of the entire United States eastern seaboard.

CHAPTER 15
The Legendary deBraak

In the year 1781, exactly two centuries prior to this writing, Dutch shipbuilders pounded out the keepblocks to send a newly constructed cutter sliding down the ways. The cutter, eighty-four feet long on deck and 125 feet overall, was christened *deBraak*, outfitted with twelve guns, and commissioned into the Admiralty of the Muese, one of the political predecessors of the modern Netherlands. Thus began a seventeen-year naval career which, under two flags, would lead to fame and controversy. Its end would come suddenly and tragically off a Delaware Cape, but its legend would endure forever and the little ship would take a prominent place in the annals of sunken treasure.

For her first fourteen years, the *deBraak* logged a record of steady, if unremarkable, service under the Dutch flag. She participated in the defense against invading French forces and made her longest voyage to Dutch Guiana (now Surinam) in South America. In 1795, yet another disturbance in the volatile political balance of Europe dramatically altered the course of her future service. While she was in the English harbor of Falmouth preparing for convoy escort duty, a revolution in Holland shifted power to the Dutch Batavian Republic, a government siding with France, with whom England was at war. The *deBraak,* in the wrong harbor at the wrong time, was seized as an "enemy" ship; a year later she was surveyed and entered onto the active naval roles of the British Admiralty. British naval designers did not favor her single-mast, fore-and-aft cutter rig and ordered modification to a brig rig. In June, 1797, the H.M.S. *deBraak,* now a British sloop of war with two masts, sixteen 24-pound carronades (a short barrel, large bore deck gun), and under the command of Lieutenant James Drew, received her first orders from the British Navy.

The account of the *deBraak* from this point until her arrival in Delaware is based upon a report prepared by Howard I. Chapelle and Lt. Col. M. E. S. Laws, R.A. (Ret.), who have taken their information only from official Admiralty records. From June to December, 1797, the *deBraak* was assigned to routine escort duty off England. Drew was then ordered to take his ship to Plymouth to refit and prepare for foreign service, namely, to join with the H.M.S. *St. Albans* for Atlantic convoy escort duty to Delaware Bay. From Delaware, the *deBraak* was to escort southbound ships to Chesapeake ports while the *St. Albans* accompanied those bound for Philadelphia, New York, and Boston. Upon completion of the mission, both warships would sail for Halifax, Nova Scotia.

On March 26, 1798, the two escorts joined their forty-four ship convoy and sailed for America. Almost two weeks later, on April 4th, several days of stormy weather scattered the convoy and the *deBraak* became separated from the other ships. Now sailing alone, the little sloop of war spied and pursued a sail which proved to be a Spanish merchantman bound from Rio de Plata, South America, to Cadiz, Spain. Drew dutifully captured the Spaniard and found aboard a cargo of cacao and a valuable shipment of 200 tons of copper ingots. A British prize crew was put on board the merchantman and some of the Spanish prisoners taken aboard the *deBraak*.

The remainder of the voyage was apparently uneventful and the two ships arrived off Cape Henlopen, the entrance to Delaware Bay, at 4:00 P.M. on May 25th. With a pilot aboard, the *deBraak* was preparing to anchor a short distance off Lewestown (now Lewes) when a sudden, intense squall bore down on the ship. What followed took only a few minutes; still under mainsail and perhaps too much topsail, the *deBraak* caught a gust of wind and heeled over. With hatches open, she filled rapidly and sank, leaving only her topgallant mastheads above the sea. The sinking, which occurred about one mile off Cape Henlopen light, took the life of Captain Drew and thirty-five others, including twelve Spanish prisoners.

After investigating the sinking, British Admiralty authorities in Philadelphia ordered the H.M.S. *Hind* and the H.M.S. *Vixen* to attempt to salvage the *deBraak* from its shallow water grave. The ships began sweeping for the wreck on September 15th, 1798; an anchor was recovered and cables attached, but the hulk could not be moved. The effort was abandoned four days later. Aside from the human tragedy, the *deBraak* represented no great loss to the British Navy, and her timbers and memories seemed destined to join those of other ships, lost and forgotten beneath the sands of the mid-Atlantic coast.

Such was not to be her fate, however, for her masts still showed above the water as other accounts of her voyage were heard. To begin, the *deBraak* had captured a prize and, with its cargo of copper ingots, a "rich" prize at that. And the prize was not French or Dutch, but a *Spanish* ship. After the sinking, many survivors settled accounts for room and board in Lewes with gold and silver Spanish coins, bemoaning the loss of the ship and implying there had been a lot more on board. The loss of the ship's log left gaping holes in the official account of the last voyage, holes that were opportunities for creative storytellers. Finally, the *deBraak* had just sunk when the British Navy attempted to salvage it, a solid indication of the existence of very valuable cargo aboard. Within a year, the *deBraak* was already becoming a legend with many versions of her now famous last voyage. A composite of some of the better ones might sound like this:

The *deBraak*, under secret orders and bearing a marque of reprisal against Spanish shipping, slipped away from her convoy and set course for the Caribbean. There, ruthless Captain Drew captured galleon after galleon, taking only treasure and no prisoners. Loaded to the gunwales with treasure, the *deBraak* then stopped at Kingston, Jamaica, to pick up a military payroll for shipment to Halifax. Upon arrival at Cape Henlopen, the ship was top-heavy with treasure and Captain Drew and his crew were drunk when a squall . . .

Such accounts had great popular appeal even though, realistically, they were absurd. If the little *deBraak* had the foolish audacity to confront a Spanish frigate, Drew's "heave to" signal would have been answered by a withering twenty-gun broadside. Still, interest in salvaging the "treasure" of the *deBraak* began almost immediately. In 1805, Gilbert McCracken, a local Lewestown harbor pilot, apparently located the wreck by dragging, and took bearings from the old lighthouse and other points of reference. His map would surface a century later to be used by modern treasure salvors. Although documentation is lacking, the British Navy is believed to have made two more salvage attempts, the last in 1814. The next major attempt at the treasure was the Pancoast Expedition, backed by wealthy New York and Philadelphia investors, in 1877.

By 1879, the "fact" that the *deBraak* sunk with a fabulous load of treasure was firmly established. Any disbelievers had only to refer to the factual article published that year by that bastion of truth, the *New York Times,* carrying, as usual, "all the news that's fit to print."

SEEKING SUNKEN MONEY
Hunting For Gold Buried In The Atlantic

LEWES, Del., April 28—. . . It has been a great many years since the wrecks in question occurred, and no doubt by this time the vessels in question are covered up by the constantly changing channels, with nothing visible to mark their resting places. It has been said that the Delaware seacoast undergoes more changes than any other ocean shore. South of Cape Henlopen, the waves of the Atlantic now roll over spots where once large islands, covered with woods, were to be seen, and where ships could once easily sail, there are now shoals, rapidly becoming islands. These freaks on the part of nature make it doubtful if the adventurers will ever set eyes on the sunken riches. But while it may be true, and it very likely is, that the money is beyond human reach, the fact that it lies there cannot be gainsaid. Its existence is proven by history and recent events. One of the most prominent cases that can be cited to this effect is the story of the French ship de Brock. The de Brock was an armed ship commanded by an American named James Drew, but manned by a French crew. She did excellent service during the early part of the Revolutionary War and made several captures. About the third or fourth year of the War she convoyed a large quantity of gold coins and arms from France to America, the arms being for the Colonial forces and the money being secretly loaned to the colonies. She was chased by several English frigates, but reached her destination in Synepuxette

Bay, near where is now situated Ocean City, Md. The money and munitions of war were landed and conveyed by wagon up the peninsula to Wilmington under escort of a company of Delaware militia commanded by Col. David Hall, accompanied by a body of French soldiers, who came over on the De Brock . . .

. . . The De Brock, after waiting in Synepuxette Bay until her English pursuers went away, stood out to sea, and in the course of two days captured two Engish prize ships which were loaded with valuable cargo and a large amount of coin. She then set sail for Lewes to take on supplies. When nearing the mouth of the Bay, Captain Drew committed the ship into the hands of Andrew Allen, one of the best pilots about Lewes in those days. She had her topsails furled and clew-lines hauled, and a stiff wind was blowing at the time. Drew, full of vanity and, it is said, also full of liquor, had all her sails set again as she prepared to round the Cape, despite Allen's remonstrance, and she capsized, filled, and went down, taking to the bottom with her the two prizes and the gold they contained in their holds. Some of the crews succeeded in getting into one of the boats and many of the drowning men swam to it, only to have their fingers and hands cut off with knives and swords, as they caught hold of the gunwales of the boat, and endeavored to climb in, and thus were left to the mercy of the waves. Very few reached shore alive. Drew was washed in lifeless, and is buried in the old Episcopal churchyard with a monument above him, the inscription upon which relates how he died. Allen survived and his story of the untold wealth that went to the bottom with the De Brock has been handed down from generation to generation, and is often related to the summer tourists by the rough old wreckers with a gusto that is quite amazing. From this wreck, much gold has from time to time been washed ashore, and it is said that a few days after the wreck, the father of William Marshall, the Lieutenant Commander of the post at Lewes during the War of 1812, and several others, secured enough of the precious metal to make them rich for the time being. These came ashore on fragments of the ship, and were picked up on the most seaward point of Cape Henlopen.

But this wreck is not the only one. Sometime between the Revolution and the War of 1812 an American brig bound from Liverpool to Baltimore, with specie on board, was wrecked on a shoal lying out from Synepuxette Beach, and there was beaten to pieces by the heavy surf. A gold laden Spanish vessel was also wrecked upon the Hen and Chicken Shoals, just off the beach south of the Cape. This is one of the most treacherous and fatal beaches upon the whole Atlantic coast. More wrecks have occurred here than upon any similar extent of shore with which the United States Life-saving service have anything to do. Upon this beach, where so often have been found the corpses of unfortunate mariners, gold and silver coin has been washed up by the waves. No later than last fall, after the terrific storm in October, two pieces of gold coin and a Spanish dollar were found near the edge of the surf . . .

Whether or not the *deBraak* had treasure on it when it sunk was irrelevant. It was a treasure ship now, for the *New York Times* had made it so while "documenting" a few of the missing details of the last voyage. Such "fact" inspired further salvage attempts and the International Submarine Company gave it a try in 1880. Then came Ocean Wrecking, Ltd., operating on capital secured through the sale of fifty-dollar stock certificates, each inscribed with the encouraging notation that the bearer was "entitled to $1,400 in case Treasures to the value of Ten Millions of Dollars shall be realized therefrom." Neither the Ocean Wrecking Company nor their investors ever realized a cent, but that did not deter Captain Jeff Townsend, of Somers Point, New Jersey, from seeking the treasure in 1888. Working with a large crew of divers from the steamer *Tamasse,* Townsend found no treasure, but something to add a bit more mystery to the legendary wreck. It was an enormous anchor chain ninety feet long, one end of which disappeared into the seabottom; neither winches nor other mechanical means could move it.

The legend grew further when U.S. Navy ships dragged up a rusted cannon while sweeping the waters off Cape Henlopen for German mines in 1917. The gun was identified as a carronade of the *deBraak* era. While many dreamed of salvaging the treasure, others, the descendents of James Drew, dreamed of clearing the Captain's name of the repeated slanderous accusations of piracy. Like the treasure salvors, they, too, failed, as shown in this 1925 article in which the *New York Times* had yet another version of the sinking of the *deBraak*.

The Braake's Treasure Still Awaits Salvage

Somewhere in the deep water off Cape Henlopen lies a treasure of a half million in British gold, and much more in gold and silver bars, plate, and other valuables. In 1798, the British privateer Braake sailed for the West Atlantic, bearing enough gold to pay off all the British troops stationed in various parts of the New World. As the soldiers had not been paid in many months, the sum was a large one.

It will never be known whether the Captain of the Braake decided to turn pirate or whether he was merely showing excessive zeal in making war on all enemies of England he met on the high seas. The fact that the Braake took no prisoners and sank every prize goes a long way toward proving the piracy theory.

The Braake captured a Spanish merchantman coming up from South American ports, transferred the precious cargo to her own hold and burned the vessel. Another Spanish vessel bringing a church service of richly jeweled gold plate to a New World cathedral encountered the privateer and suffered the same fate. The next to fall victim to the Braake's rapacity was a Frenchman carrying silks, spices, brandy, and bars of gold and silver, and that, too, was sent to the bottom after it had been despoiled. At last the Braake was overtaken by a hurricane when nearing the American coast, was blown far out of her course and sank near Cape Henlopen.

Several of her crew escaped in a small boat and reached land. Their tales of treasure on the sunken ship caused expeditions to be fitted out, but nothing was brought up except pieces of the anchor chain and a cannon or two. During the last 100 years, every effort to raise the treasure has failed.

The last attempt was made by Commander Charles Adams, U.S.N., who fitted out a ship under the auspices of the Navy Department, but was unable to locate the wreck which, by this time, is thought to be deeply submerged in the ooze and slime of the ocean bed.

The 1930s saw steady work by a number of salvage groups seeking the treasure of the *deBraak*. In 1932–33, representatives from Merritt, Chapman, and Scott, the oldest salvage firm in the United States, formed the Braak Corporation. Using the most modern equipment available, even these experts found only disappointment as reported by the Wilmington (Delaware) *Morning News*.

SUNKEN GOLD QUEST ENDS AS BRAKKE COMPANY DIES

Randolph McCracken, Lewes Butcher, Is Sad But Still Has Hopes of Treasure From Old Sloop That Took His Grandfather To Death

LEWES, July 6—Another group of treasure hunters has given up the search for the British sloop of war *de Braak* which, with its reputed $800,000 in Spanish gold now lying at the bottom of the Delaware Bay near Cape Henlopen, has eluded salvagers for 138 years.

The Braak Corporation, which in 1932 conducted the most elaborate and well equipped search ever made for the sunken sloop, has decided to let the company "die a natural death" . . .

. . . The old Fire Island Lightship was purchased and outfitted with the most modern salvaging devices to resume operations in 1933. But the Bank holiday intervened. People became afraid to risk capital. The lightship, renamed the "Drew" after the skipper of the ill-fated deBraak, never steamed into the Delaware breakwater.

Randolph McCracken, 61 year old butcher

and grandson of Gilbert McCracken, who piloted the sloop to her last anchorage on May 31, 1798, was disconsolate when he learned of the abandonment. He alone of all the residents in this seafaring town shows any great interest in a salvage claim. His belief that he would someday inherit the undersea legacy has never faltered, despite the long history of failures dating from 1805.

Socialites Try And Fail

Last Summer a group of Providence, Rhode Island, sportsmen and socialites headed by Richard T. Wilson and working under the direction of Charles N. Colstad of Attleboro, Mass., made a preliminary search.

Satisfied that they had found the location of the little sloop, only 125 feet long and with a 30 foot beam, they chartered the former

Boston pilot schooner Liberty, and returned to Lewes in late summer. Stormy weather and an unseasonable early autumn called a halt.

Both Colstad and Wilson said they would return this spring to raise the vessel, if possible, and bring her cargo of gold coins, Spanish doubloons and pieces of eight to the surface, as well as deckload of copper she is reported to have been carrying.

The summer is a third gone. The squally season will arrive in about three weeks, and still no sign of a salvage ship. McCracken, saddened by the end of the Braak Corporation, still keeps his chart beneath (?) his pilot ancestor. Daily he walks to the waterfront to talk over the possibilities with others and to scan the horizon for a sight of the "Liberty", which to him spells "Hope".

McCracken's hope came not as the *Liberty,* but as a smaller craft. When work finally began it lasted through the summer and made treasure the daily topic of conversation in bars and along the waterfront.

Fishing Parties View the Treasure Hunt

LEWES, Sept. 4—Fishing parties at the Delaware Capes the past ten days have turned into sight seeing expeditions to view the operations of the salvage vessels which are endeavoring to recover the reputed millions in gold from the sunken sloop deBraak, it was revealed here today by owners of party boats.

Attracted by the diving equipment on the Nellie L. Paramenter, 45 foot salvage ship, and the wrecking launch Doubloons, now operating at the Cam buoy at the entrance to the Delaware breakwaters, most fishing parties request that the skippers "heave to" when passing near the boats so they may have a close view of any treasure that is brought up from the sea.

> So far nary a doubloon or piece of eight
> has been sighted by curious spectators, but
> Charles N. Colstad, leader of the expedition,
> and Diver Jack Talty are careful to see that no
> revealing evidence is brought to the surface
> when other vessels are standing by.

While the Colstad attempt failed to find the treasure, others simply had to walk to the nearby beaches to find some.

OLD COINS FOUND AT LEWES

LEWES, Oct. 6—The copper coins found on the beach near Cape Henlopen following the tropical hurricane are believed to be from a secret cache buried by either of two famous pirates, Captain Kidd or Levi West, the local buccaneer. Old documents show both pirates operated in this section. Dozens of copper coins have been found during the past two weeks by fishermen.

These copper coins were actually found ten miles to the south and had nothing to do with pirates or the wreck of the *deBraak* (see Chapter 17), but were uncovered by the constant shifting of the beach sands. In 1937, the idea of sand movement gave birth to yet another approach to find the treasure. Captain Jim Bartlett's theory placed the wreck of the *deBraak* directly beneath the beach, thus best located by a core drilling or a well drilling machine. Although the core drilling idea was never tested, Bartlett contributed his share to the still growing legend. Thirty years earlier (1907), Bartlett said he had seen a black preacher named Davis pick up a gold brick, worn thin and nicked. Bartlett accompanied Davis to the United States Mint at Philadelphia where the brick was sold for $140. Bartlett believed there were thirteen more gold bars in Drew's quarters aboard the *deBraak*, "since he took two for each of the Spanish ships he captured."

The salvage attempts continued through the 1950s and 1960s with both local groups and Philadelphia interests giving it their best, seeking a treasure and, at the same time, enhancing and perpetuating a magnificent legend. Rusted iron shipboard fittings were dredged up and claimed to have come from the *deBraak.* Some of the most encouraging recoveries were pieces of waterlogged teak that supposedly came from the deck of the *deBraak.* The salvors' enthusiasm was not the least diminished when marine historians agreed that the ship had been constructed almost entirely of oak. In March, 1971, *Saga* magazine, a men's adventure publication, printed a particularly lusty version of the sinking of the *deBraak,* upping the value of the treasure considerably. The article, written by Al Masters, was titled *Delaware's $40 Million Treasure Jinx,* and was followed by this lengthy subheading:

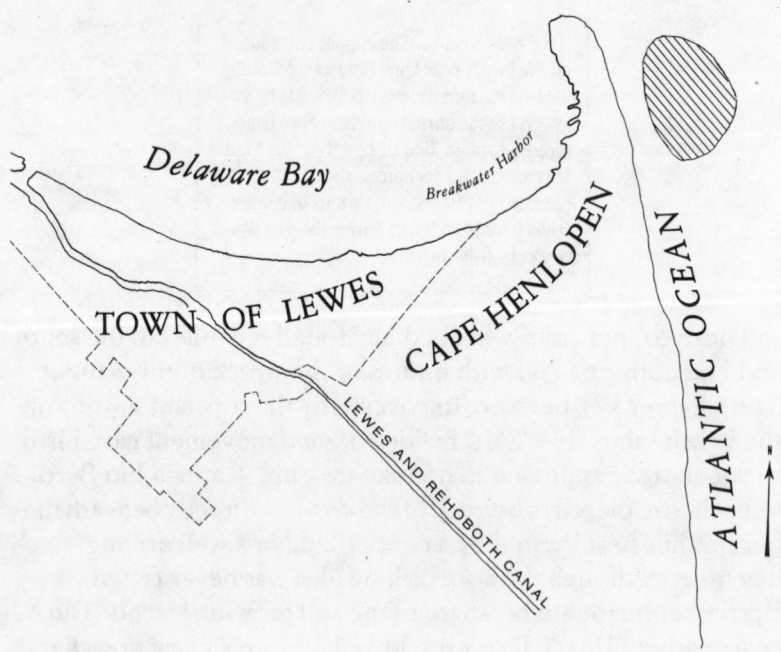

Cape Henlopen as it appears today. Lined area indicates general location of the wreck of the H.M.S. *deBraak.*

Thoroughly documented in English Admiralty archives, the *deBraak,* a one-masted sloop of war, was so jammed with booty that the loot from its last prize had to be lashed to its deck. That probably was its undoing, because in a severe storm off Cape Henlopen, the cargo shifted and the vessel capsized in only fourteen fathoms of water. Since that disaster on May 25th, 1798, the deadly tides and unpredictable weather have defeated no fewer than thirteen expeditions . . .

Salvage attempts on the *deBraak* continued into the early 1970s. In 1979, one salvor was informed by the Admiralty in London that the British still claimed a portion of any treasure should it be salvaged. The most recent try came in 1980 as a local backer got together with a Florida treasure salvage company. They, too, like the more than twenty expeditions over 183 years before them, failed.

Since the day when the *deBraak* heeled over and sank, the Delaware coast has undergone great change. Cape Henlopen has built northward in the shape of a delicate hook at least one mile beyond its 1798 limit, while the beach line has migrated westward. Treasure hunters, with their dreams and equipment, have come and gone over the years, while the town of Lewes has remained a picturesque and perfect keeper for the *deBraak* legends. It is still a port, not for the brigs and frigates of history, but now for fishing boats, pleasure craft, and the ferries that connect Delaware with New Jersey's Cape May. History lives in Lewes, in its centuries old graveyards and along the waterfront where old iron cannon still point seaward. Much of the local lore and legend rests in the Zwaanandael Museum, an elaborately gabled building designed as a replica of a Dutch town hall. In a quiet alcove is an exhibit devoted to the H.M.S. *deBraak.* A model of the little sloop of war is backed by framed news clippings telling of salvage attempts and charts of the wreck area. On the floor is an old wooden trunk, believed to be the personal property of Captain James Drew, Royal Navy, and upon which three surviving Spanish prisoners reportedly floated to the beach after the sinking.

Only two blocks away from the Zwaanandael Museum, the bones of Captain James Drew rest in St. Peter's Episcopal Churchyard beneath a tall stone memorial erected by his widow. Upon it are engraved the following words:

Part of the *deBraak* exhibit in the Zwaanandael Museum, Lewes, DE, showing Captain Drew's trunk and a hull model of the sloop of war.

Here Rest
the remains of
CAPTAIN JAMES DREW
who commanded
HIS BRITANNIC MAJESTY'S
sloop of war deBraak
in which he lost his life
when she foundered at the
Capes of Delaware
the 10th of June 1798
He was beloved for his virtues
and admired for his bravery
His affectionate Relict
has erected this Monument
to perpetuate his
MEMORY

   Why the date June 10th appears, instead of the documented date of the sinking, May 25, has never been explained. The stone vase atop the monument is reported to have been sent by Queen Anne. A few steps away in the quiet, tree shaded graveyard are two stones bearing the name McCracken. One marks the grave of Gilbert McCracken, who took the bearings to the wreck in 1805, the other is his son, Henry F., also a Delaware Bay and River Pilot, who requested that he be buried with his anchor. His request was granted, and the rusted fluke of the anchor may be seen protruding above the ground.

   Three miles from Lewes is the Atlantic beach which looks just as it did on May 25th, 1798, when a gallant little sloop of war named the H.M.S. *deBraak* heeled over and sank to become one of the greatest of all sunken treasure legends.

CHAPTER 16
The Wreck of the Faithful Steward

The welcome peace following the Revolution brought a sharp increase in the numbers of European immigrants eager to escape Old World social and economic depression. Most of those who sailed to the young United States were initially of English, Irish, or Scottish ancestry, people familiar with the culture and language and hoping to join friends and relatives who had immigrated earlier.

Most of the immigrants adopted the same personal pattern of financial preparation. Since neither trans-Atlantic banking channels nor acceptable, negotiable paper instruments existed, nor could the average man yet ship any quantity of material possessions, there remained but one way to transfer wealth. Immigrants converted their worldly belongings into gold and silver coinage, the nationality of which mattered little. For thousands of immigrants, the stake for the future was a small leather pouch of English guineas, Portuguese Johannas, or Spanish escudos.

In 1785, the *Faithful Steward* was typical of the ships in the growing fleet of merchantmen that carried the immigrants to their new home. Although documentation is not available, she was probably about 150 feet long with a three-masted ship rig. On what was to be her last voyage, she departed Londonderry, Ireland, in mid-July, bound for Philadelphia. Crowded into her dismal quarters were 249 passengers, one hundred of whom were women and children. In her holds was a miscellaneous cargo of general trade goods including a large consignment of copper coins.

The coins were English and Irish halfpennies, the mass circulation "coppers" that had an interesting numismatic background.

117

England minted prodigious quantities of the coins for use both at home and throughout its empire. When the English found themselves with an overproduction of coinage, they frequently pressured the Irish to accept them for circulation. If the Irish rejected the coins, the next stop for the kegs of coppers was most likely to be the American colonies which had always been plagued by a shortage of metallic coinage. Even after independence, the young United States suffered a similar plight for decades. The Irish sometimes found cause to reject the coinage for more than the usual political or economic reasons. On several occasions, the English minted coins for the Irish that were underweight and undersize. One such shipment, minted in 1722 but predated to 1700, was brought to public attention by a W. B. Drapier, the pseudonym for the prominent writer Jonathan Swift. Whatever the reason for the large consignment of coppers aboard the *Faithful Steward,* the ex-colonies were the place to get rid of them.

The *Faithful Steward* was about to complete her uneventful Atlantic crossing on September 1, 1785. Position sightings placed the ship very near the entrance to Delaware Bay but, by evening, land had not yet been sighted. Arrival on the coast was the most critical part of the voyage, and it was vital that land be sighted at the earliest possible time. A few hours after dark the Captain ordered soundings taken and was appalled to find the ship in only four fathoms—twenty-four feet—of water. All hands were called to help turn the ship, hoping to clear the shoals and sail to the east, then lay to until dawn. Despite every effort, the hull brushed the sand, then grounded. The wind and sea were rising, and the ship was finally lightened by cutting away the mainmast. But even after clearing the shoals, the *Faithful Steward* found it could not beat against the increasing wind.

At dawn on September 2nd, she was aground again, this time on the shoals directly off the Delaware beach about four leagues—ten miles—south of Cape Henlopen, and totally helpless before a major storm, probably a tropical hurricane. The beach meant safety, but it was 150 yards away, and swimming or rowing through thundering breakers was impossible. Word of "Ship ashore!" reached nearby Lewestown and residents gathered at the beach, unable to do anything but watch the developing catastrophe. With each crashing wave that exploded around the *Faithful Steward,* the keel settled deeper in the sand, placing more and more stress upon the hull. From the beach, observers could plainly hear the screams from the 270 helpless souls who crowded the deck of the doomed ship.

Had this shoaling occurred a century later, it is probable that all would have been saved. The Life Saving Service would somehow have gotten a line aboard, perhaps even reached the ship in a surfboat. But the year was 1785 and the 270 aboard the *Faithful Steward* were on their own. Because of the list and position of the ship, the small boats on board were launched with great difficulty, and the turmoil of the sea prevented the passengers and crew from boarding them. Every boat capsized, drifting to shore empty. By evening, the storm peaked and the hull of the *Faithful Steward* could take no more. The ship began breaking up; within hours the sea completed its work.

The seas still ran very high at dawn on September 3rd, and all that remained of the *Faithful Steward* were the planks, timbers, rigging, and wreckage that littered the beach along with the bodies of the dead. Out of the one hundred women and children, ninety-three washed ashore drowned. Four out of every five persons aboard perished.

When the *Faithful Steward* broke up, she dropped her coins and other cargo atop another wreck, that of the *Three Brothers,* which was lost under identical circumstances ten years earlier. It was widely believed that the *Three Brothers* carried a military payroll of gold, silver, and copper coins destined for the British command at Philadelphia. The cargos of both ships were dropped to the sea bottom to become a part of the shifting sands, and nothing remained off the lonely Delaware beach to mark the site of the tragedies. But many decades later, the sea would begin to give back what it had claimed on that September day in 1785 and, once again, people would remember the *Faithful Steward.*

CHAPTER 17
The Delaware Coin Beach

The sinking of the *Faithful Steward,* of course, was an insignificant event in the formation and reformation of the beach; the sands moved continuously, always toward the west and south. No one remembers when the first coins were found on the beach, but it was probably the late 1800s when someone picked up from the surf line a corroded copper coin and rubbed it to reveal the image of King George III. Those first coins were merely considered "old" and were attributed to no particular wreck, as locations of the sinkings had been long forgotten. More and more of the coins appeared and, by 1920, the beach just north of the Indian River Inlet was already known as "Coin Beach."

The Delaware coin beach, looking north from the Indian River Inlet Bridge. This section of beach has probably yielded more historic coins than any other in the nation.

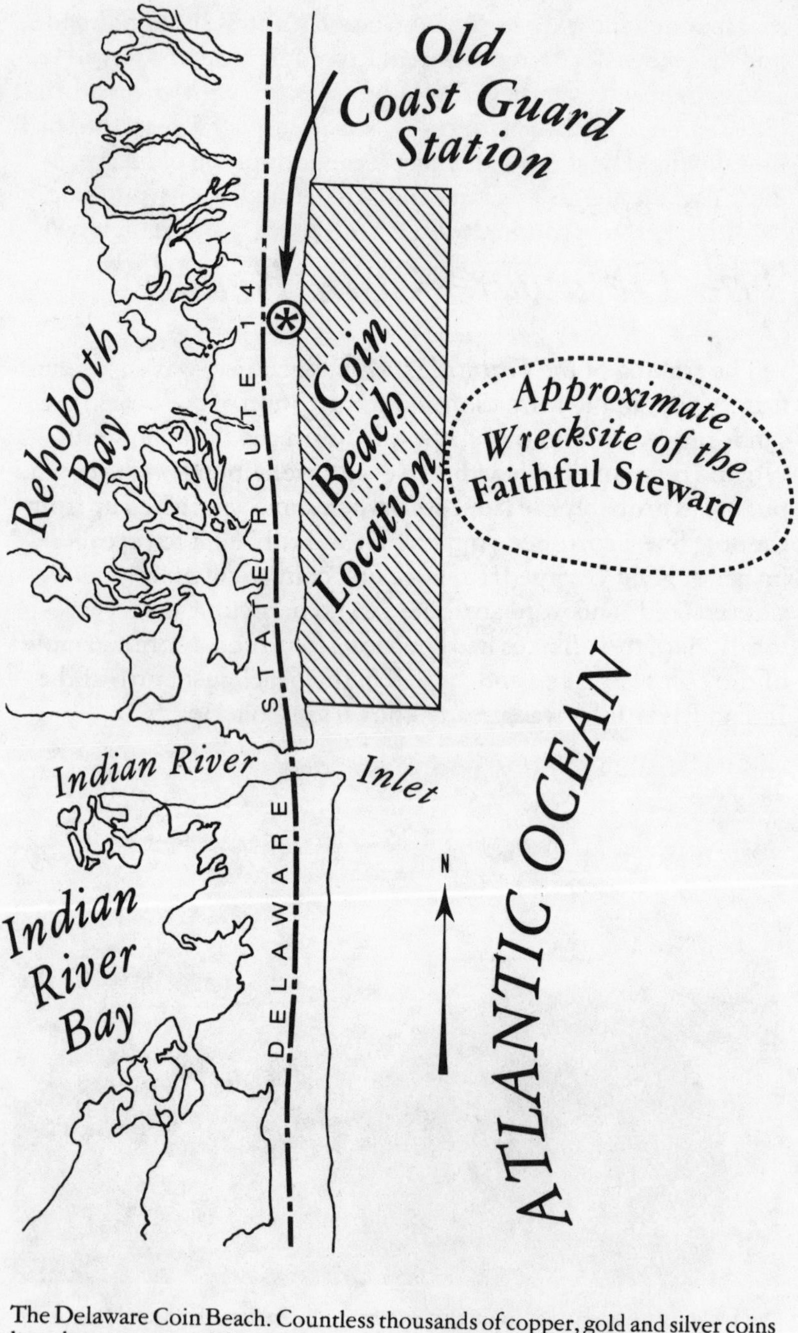

Old
Coast Guard
Station

Coin
Beach
Location

Approximate
Wrecksite of the
Faithful Steward

Rehoboth
Bay

STATE ROUTE 14

DELAWARE

Indian River

Inlet

Indian
River
Bay

N

ATLANTIC OCEAN

The Delaware Coin Beach. Countless thousands of copper, gold and silver coins have been recovered from the section indicated. Coins are now even being recovered to the south of the Indian River Inlet.

During the 1930s, the United States Coast Guard personnel that manned the old Life Saving Station located about one and one half miles north of the Indian River Inlet found a way to amuse themselves at their desolate post. After each severe storm, they searched the beach for coins, and after several years they had literally filled buckets with many thousands of the old halfpennies. The number is by no means exaggerated, for by this time, organized groups routinely visited the beach to stage their own treasure hunts, as reported by this *New York Times* article in 1937.

FIND
GEORGE III
COINS
CCC Boys Gather Hundreds Of
Coppers On Delaware Beach

LEWES, Del., Feb. 23 (AP).—Copper coins issued under the reign of George III of Great Britain and bearing dates from 1774 to 1782 were picked up along the ocean front today near Indian River Inlet, just south of Lewes.

Youths from the Lewes CCC camp discovered several hundred coins lying on the beach yesterday and a holiday treasure hunt revealed more.

The image of George III on an English copper halfpenny found on the Delaware coin beach.

Others joined the CCC boys as they busily filled their pockets with the old halfpennies. Sometimes the sea even gave up more than coins.

Coins of 1749-1775 Tossed Up on Beach
More Old Coppers Are Found At Lewes, Del.
Ancient Sea Chest Is Buried In Sand

Lewes, Del., March 13.—The ocean tossed two copper coins, one minted during the reign of George II of England, at the feet of Major Lindsley D. Beach, U.S.A. retired, as he was walking along the beach front.

The George II coin, dated 1749, and believed to be the oldest of many discovered between Rehoboth and the Indian River Inlet ten miles south, during the past few years, and another, dated 1775, will be added to a collection of nearly 100 found this winter by the major.

Major Beach, whose discovery three weeks ago of an ancient copper-bound sea chest, heavily encrusted with barnacles and buried deep within the sand, has attracted hundreds of treasure seekers from nearby States, is awaiting a good, stiff northeast blow before making further salvage attempts.

The shifting sand has completely covered the chest, which is about three feet square, and weighs about 400 pounds. A third of the chest was exposed in the latest northeast storm, when the winds leveled tons of sand along the entire ocean front.

It is estimated by local residents that a severe northeaster alters the height of the sand as much as four feet, but the sand quickly builds up again, often reaching its normal level within two days.

Major Beach, whose attempts to remove the chest were halted by an incoming tide, is confident of its ultimate recovery. Even if the chest does not reveal any treasure when opened, it will be valuable because of its antiquity, he believes.

The chest never seems to have reappeared, but the Delaware coin beach continued to attract treasure hunters from afar, not only because of coppers and mysterious chests, but because some of the coins were gold and silver. Most of the silver coins were Spanish pillar dollars; the gold coins were English Rose guineas minted during the reigns of George II and George III.

For decades, the source of the coins was automatically assumed to be the wreck of the *deBraak* ten miles to the north. Now it is known the coppers were the cargo of the *Faithful Steward;* the gold and silver coins may also come from that wreck as well as that of the *Three Brothers.* Most of the treasure hunters who visit the beach are equipped with modern metal detectors and are successful. The copper halfpennies are bought and sold locally for five dollars to ten dollars, depending upon condition. The Spanish pillar dollars bring several hundred dollars each, and the gold Rose guineas as much as $5,000. Further inspiration for treasure hunters may be found at the Zwaanandael Museum in Lewes, where an exhibit of beach coins is displayed in a glass case upon a beach-like scattering of sand. Included among the coppers is a gleaming English gold Rose guinea recovered from the same beach.

A gold English rose guinea on display in the Zwaanandael Museum, Lewes, DE. This coin, worth about $5,000, was recovered on the Delaware coin beach.

Recently at the Zwaanandael, the curator casually produced for a visitor a sack containing several hundred of the old copper halfpennies that had been donated by local beachcombers. The coins vary greatly in condition, but on each could be seen either the King's image and the English coat of arms or the distinctive Irish harp design. To touch those coins is to bridge the two centuries that have slipped away since the *Faithful Steward* broke up on a Delaware beach. Again, the sea had given back a little of its treasure. Perhaps, some day, it may even give back the Major's sea chest.

PART V

Maryland-Virginia Eastern Shore Treasures

CHAPTER 18

The Eastern Shore

From the Fenwick Island Lighthouse at the Delaware-Maryland state line, to Cape Charles on the northern approach to Chesapeake Bay, are ninety miles of barrier beaches and islands that make up the eastern shore. Only two lighthouses mark the coast. Assateague Light was built in 1833 and stands at the southern end of Assateague Island. The original structure served until it was replaced by a more powerful beacon atop a new 142-foot stone tower in 1867. The Cape Charles Light was built in 1828 on isolated Smith Island. Construction of a new tower was practically completed when Rebel guerillas captured the island; progress was set back two years and the new light finally went into service in 1864 under a Union military guard. Still another tower had to be built in 1895 in another part of the island not threatened by beach erosion. By 1880, five lifesaving stations had been established on the eastern shore, one at Ocean City, Maryland, and the others along the Virginia barrier islands—some of the most remote stations in the entire national system. The stations had their work cut out for them, for historians estimate that well over 600 ships have wrecked along the eastern shore.

The eastern shore differs from the remainder of the densely populated mid-Atlantic, for only one section, that near Ocean City, has undergone intensive development. That building boom was a direct result of the March storm of 1962, itself a mid-Atlantic legend, which created the present Ocean City Inlet, and enhanced regional recreational potential and land values. The rest of the eastern shore is unspoiled and considered the Atlantic's "last frontier." Across the inlet from busy Ocean City is Assateague Island, a thirty-four mile long natural barrier island preserved as a park and refuge. Below Assateague Island, the remaining fifty miles of the eastern shore are completely undeveloped and not accessible by land at all. Much of this section is part of the Virginia Coast Reserve and under management and ownership of the Nature Conservancy. The nine major barrier islands are steeped in lore of wrecks and pirates that is reflected in their names—Wreck Island, Ship Shoal Island, and Cedar Island which, on early charts, was known as "Teches'" or "Teaches" Island. Captain Edward Teach and some of his followers did indeed use these islands as a base from which to plunder shipping in the approaches to the Chesapeake. Even today, a point of land in the shadow of Cape Charles Light on Smith Island is named for Blackbeard.

Without the presence of jetties and stabilization works, the coast here is constantly in a state of natural reformation. One of the more spectacular examples of sand movement took place at the turn of the century on Parramour Island. Returning from a Caribbean voyage in 1888, the 140-foot schooner *Esk* was caught in a severe storm, apparently a hurricane, during September 7–8. Two years later, after no sign of the vessel or her crew had ever turned up, the *Esk* was declared lost with all hands. Over a decade later, a particularly violent northeast storm struck the eastern shore, driving the sea over the low dunes and moving an enormous amount of sand. At the height of the storm, the crew of the Parramour Island Life Saving Station was shocked to see a large schooner with shattered masts moving toward the bar two hundred yards offshore. When the storm had subsided, the ship lay grounded inside the bar in fifteen feet of water. Captain Donald Stewart, a local marine historian, prepared a report on the incident many years later, describing the eerie reappearance of the ship to the life saving crew in 1900.

> . . . A boat was launched to inspect the wreck more closely. She was covered with growth, worms had attacked her decks, and it was only when her name board was found still attached, that chills probably ran up their spines—cut deeply into the pine board was the name *Esk*. Like a ghost from the past, she had finally come up from the bottom of the sea to reveal what her fate had been . . .

One of the most popular shipwreck legends of the eastern shore deals with the origin of the famous wild ponies of Assateague Island. According to one version, the ponies swam ashore

from a Spanish ship that broke up on the shoals in 1820.
Oldtimers find confirmation of the tale in the local place names of
Spanish Point and Spanish Bar that supposedly derive from the
wreck. While the tale certainly has appeal, most historians believe the ponies are descended from stock brought to Assateague
to graze in pirate and Revolutionary War days.

Among the local pirate legends, one stands clearly above all
others and tells the story of Charles Wilson, a South Carolina sea
captain who succumbed to the lure of quick wealth and turned to
piracy in 1740. His career was predictable; he was finally captured, taken to London in chains, tried and found guilty of piracy,
and hanged. While awaiting death in London, he wrote a letter to
his brother, George, who still resided in Charleston, South
Carolina. The letter was apparently confiscated from the condemned pirate and filed in the voluminous British naval records
where it remained for 198 years until found and made public in
1948.

The Year 1750
London, England

To my Brother, George Wilson,
*There are three creeks lying 100 paces or more north of the second
inlet above Chincoteague Island, which is at the south end of the
peninsula. At the head of the third creek to the northward is a
bluff facing the Atlantic Ocean with three cedar trees growing on
it, each about one and one-third yards apart. Between the trees I
buried ten iron-bound chests, bars of silver, gold, diamonds, and
jewels to the sum of 200,000 sterling. Go to the woody knoll and
remove the treasure.*

With details like that, one might think that recovering the
treasure would be a simple matter of digging it up. When the
letter became public knowledge, many groups raced to the
desolate reaches of Assateague Island to do just that, only to find
the island had undergone such enormous change as to make the
letter and early charts useless. Since the time of Wilson's adventure in piracy, as many as eleven inlets have been cut through

the long barrier island, some silting over, others remaining open. The mass of the island itself has migrated westward and at low tide in some sections can be seen the remains of blackened stumps that were once cedar forests. Wilson's treasure is still sought today and takes its place with the coin beaches and wrecks as part of the treasure lore of the eastern shore. Incidentally, Wilson's 200,000 pounds might be worth as much as ten million dollars today.

CHAPTER 19

The 1750 Spanish Treasure Fleet

In the year 1750, while condemned pirate Charles Wilson was writing his now famous letter, other events were taking place that would bring far more treasure to the eastern shore. In Havana, Cuba, the annual homebound Spanish treasure fleet was assembling with arrivals of ships from both South America and Mexico, and the harbor beneath the great stone walls of Morro Castle bristled with activity as ten ships made final preparations for the long voyage to Spain.

The Spanish had adhered rigidly to their *flota* system for centuries. Before the favorable spring winds, the Caribbean treasure ships usually arrived in Havana in May, after which every effort was made to get the combined fleet on its way as soon as possible to avoid the onset of the dreaded hurricane season. The best time for a safe and fast eastward crossing was from May through July, months usually free of hurricanes and north Atlantic storms. The Spaniards had long learned to fear the hurricanes; during their great New World colonial adventure they had lost hundreds of ships, thousands of men, and uncountable millions in treasure. Entire fleets had been wrecked in the unpredictable tropical storms. Among the most recent in the memory of those who worked to prepare the 1750 fleet for sailing were the disasters of the 1715 and 1733 fleets which littered the Florida beaches with wreckage and treasure.

The Spanish were rarely successful in getting the fleets off to a timely start. Maintenance and repair of the decrepit ships often took longer than expected, and sailing orders from the ponderous Spanish bureaucracy always seemed to be issued late. The 1750 fleet fared no better, for it was already early August when the ten ships departed Havana and committed themselves to the

Florida Straits. Several days later, the Straits were behind them as they entered the open Atlantic, the voyage just beginning. The experienced seamen soon looked uneasily to the south when winds calmed and the seas became glassy beneath a milky sky, the ominous and unmistakable signs of the approach of a hurricane. Their worst fears were realized as winds and sea steadily increased and the ships had no recourse but to shorten sail and run before the storm. The first ship to fall victim to the hurricane did so quickly and was driven ashore on a north Florida beach. The next four to meet disaster did so on the Carolina coast near Hatteras. Only two of the ships, the *Nuestra Senora de Guadalupe* and the *Zumaca* found safety in Chesapeake Bay and reached Norfolk, Virginia. The remaining ships were scattered and driven further north until, one by one, they were wrecked on the eastern shore. In *Shipwrecks of the Western Hemisphere,* Robert Marx places the wreck of the *Nuestra Senora de los Godos* "near Cape Charles" and that of the *La Galga* about fifteen leagues, or forty miles, north of Cape Charles. Such locations are, of course, very general, as the survivors themselves would have been unable to pinpoint the wrecksites of their ships on the strange coast.

Today, the northernmost wrecks of the 1750 treasure fleet are the target of a professional salvage project. Local interest was first stimulated by recurring finds of Spanish silver coins in the vicinity of Ocean City and the northern end of Assateague Island. Research since conducted in the Archives of the Indies in Seville, Spain, has linked the coins to one of the 1750 wrecks; specifically, to one of the major ships, a sixty gun warship bearing a treasure cargo which is today worth nearly $40,000,000. The research also revealed a bit of the plight of the survivors who managed to cross the bay and make a difficult overland trek to the English colonial settlement of Snow Hill, Maryland. A recently-formed salvage corporation is now going about the business of search and survey. Aside from the general information provided in news releases, the operation is being conducted quietly for fear "others may try to cash in" on the venture.

If the wreck in question does prove to be the sixty-gun warship from the 1750 fleet, a second similar wreck could be located nearby. Although it is intriguing to imagine diving to a Spanish wreck, such adventures are a bit beyond the average diver's budget. The company that is now seeking the Spanish wrecks must first raise a small fortune in itself—$500,000—to fund the project.

CHAPTER 20

Eastern Shore Coin Beaches

NORTH BEACH

On early charts, "North Beach" referred to what was then the northern end of the Assateague Peninsula near the small coastal settlement of Ocean City. Since the opening of the Ocean City Inlet in 1962 and the subsequent development boom, North Beach, in name and soul, has been lost in the growing sprawl of Ocean City where, today, long rows of hotels and condominiums stand like sentries along the once lonely beach. The beach here undergoes serious erosion and huge quantities of sand are shifted in every northeast storm of winter. While beachfront property owners are naturally concerned by the erosion, local treasure hunters look forward to the northeasters after which conditions are excellent for searching the beaches. The old coins began appearing on the local beaches in the late 1880s and, by 1936, enough had been found to warrant mention in the *New York Times*.

> ## MARYLAND BEACH YIELDS OLD COINS
>
> OCEAN CITY, Md., Dec. 27 (AP).—New finds of old Spanish coins have been found along the beach north of here and have brought some talk in favor of organizing an expedition to search for the shipwreck and pirate gold in the area . . .

The article was prophetic, even if forty-five years premature, for the recoveries of Spanish silver finally has led salvors to seek the wrecks of the 1750 Spanish treasure fleet which have probably been the source of most of the coins. While coins have been recovered along much of the northern end of Assateague, the greatest success has come on the beaches from the inlet to a point about two miles north. Copper, silver, and gold coins from many nations have been found, but most "North Beach" recoveries are Spanish silver pieces dating from the mid-1700s to the early 1800s.

Should any prospective treasure hunter need proof of the existence of the Ocean City beach coins, he or she should visit the Ocean City Lifesaving Station Museum which is housed in the ninety-year-old original Life Saving Station building on the inlet.

The Ocean City Life Saving Station Museum, Ocean City, MD, houses one of the best exhibits of early lifesaving equipment on the Atlantic coast.

Their display of Spanish silver found on local beaches includes two, four, and eight reale pieces, almost all in remarkable condition. Several pillar dollars minted in Potosi, South America, and Mexico City, and bearing the image of Charles III, are outstanding specimens. The value of each would be over five hundred dollars. Other attractions include the mid-Atlantic region's best lifesaving exhibit, with surf boats, metal surf cars, breeches buoys, line firing carronades, and early photographs of the days

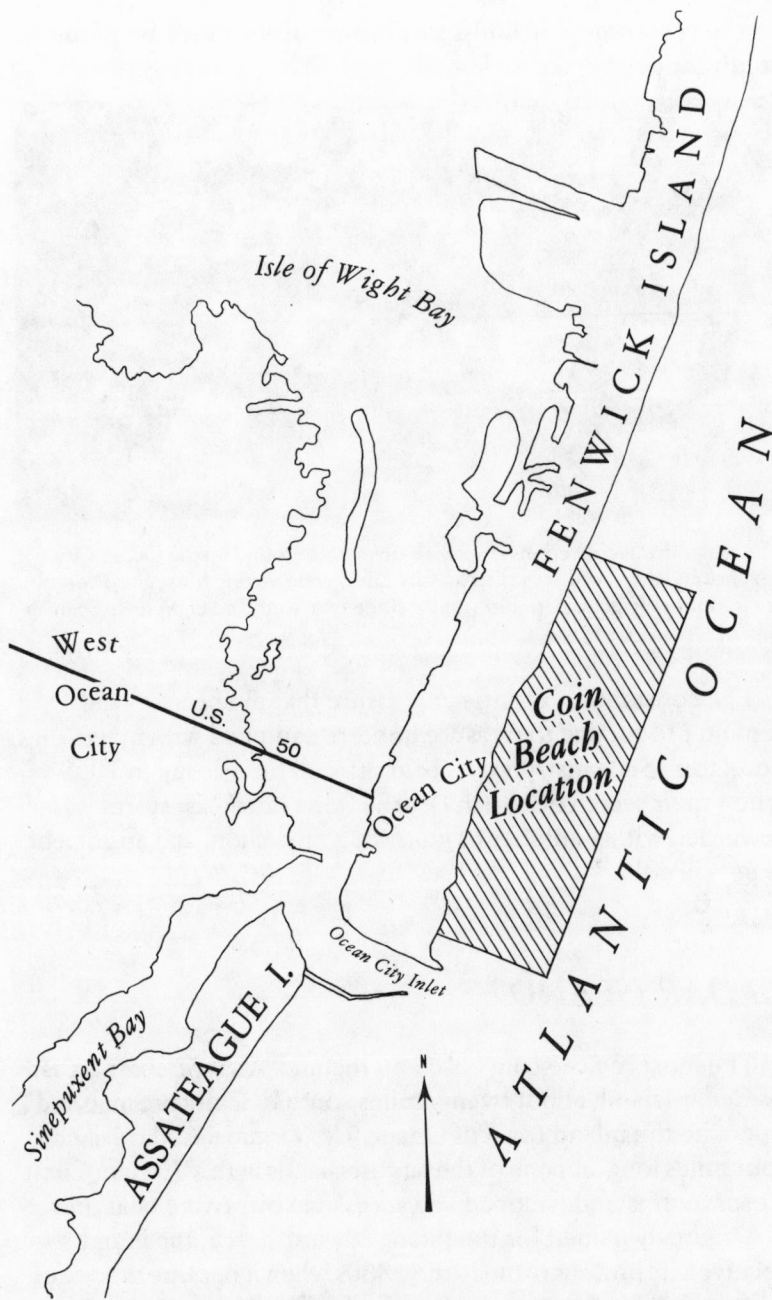

The old "North Beach" area. Spanish silver coins have been recovered in quantity from the northern end of Assateague Island to a point about two miles north of the Ocean City Inlet. The same area is also believed to be the location of a 1750 Spanish treasure wreck.

on the coast when the lifesaving crews earned every bit of the credit they received.

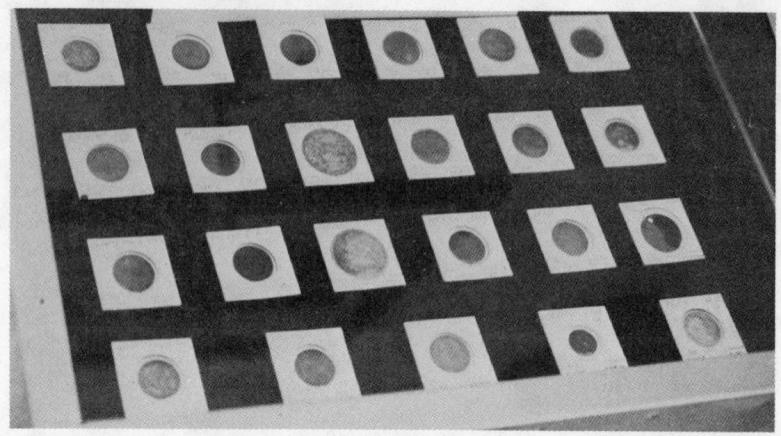

The magnificent collection of Spanish silver coins found on the Ocean City beaches and displayed at the Ocean City Life Saving Station Museum. The coins are in unusually good condition and include two, four, and eight reale Spanish silver pieces.

The constantly shifting sands assure that the beaches will remain productive to treasure hunters equipped with metal detectors. Such instruments paid off well for a group in 1968 when their search of North Beach after a northeast storm was rewarded with a number of guineas, a medallion, and an ancient ring—all gold.

CEDAR ISLAND

The most remote coin beach on the mid-Atlantic coast is that of Cedar Island, about twenty miles south of Chincoteague and opposite the inland town of Onancock, Virginia. Cedar Island is four miles long and one of the largest islands in the Virginia Coast Reserve. It is undeveloped and accessible by private boat only.

Originally named for the pirate Edward Teach, the island received its present name in the 1880s when it became the site of a lifesaving station and a hunting and fishing lodge. The first of the Cedar Island beach coins were found during these years, but not in numbers great enough to arouse serious interest. As the storms continued to turn the sands over, the coins became much

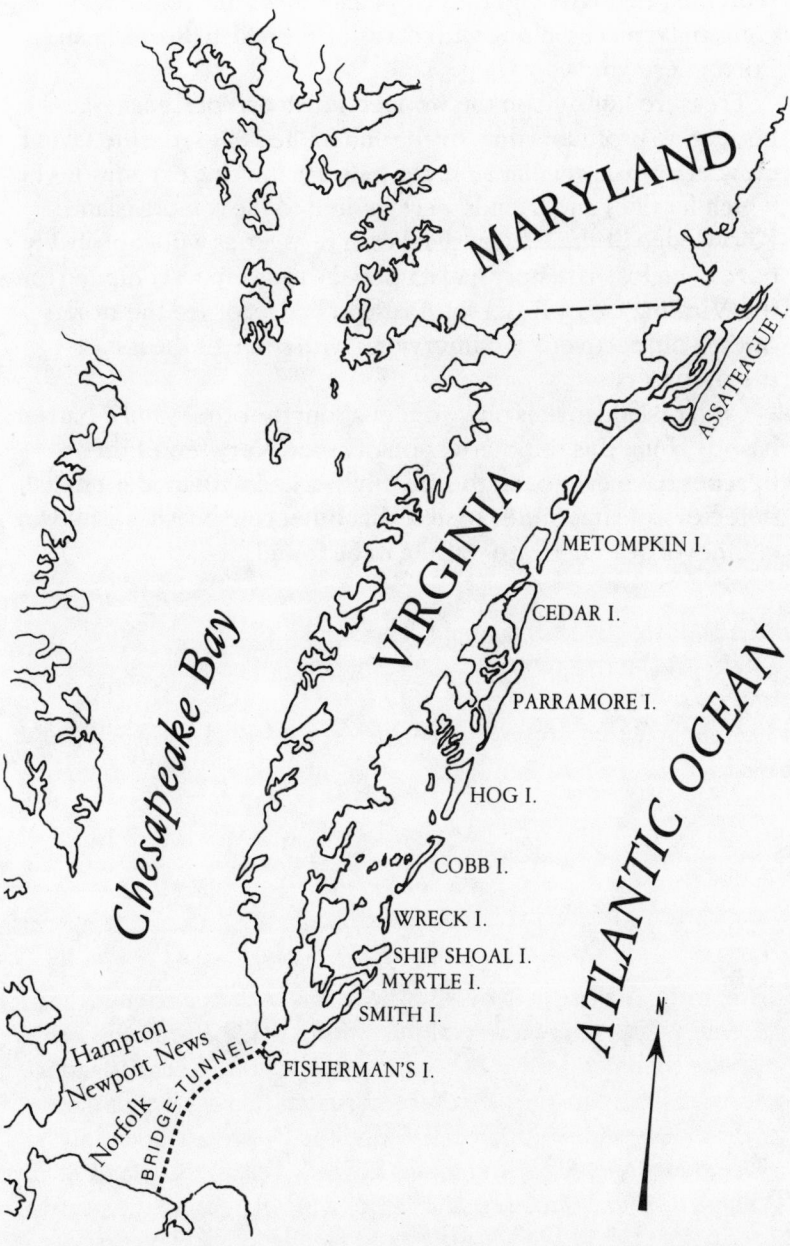

The Eastern Shore of Virginia, showing the location of Cedar Island and the other major barrier islands which would be prime areas to discover new coin beaches.

more common in the 1890s; life saving station crewmen began searching regularly and found Spanish silver in two, four, and eight reale pieces, along with occasional English, Spanish, and Portuguese gold coins.

Treasure hunting on the wooded north end of Cedar Island became so profitable that, by the end of the 1890s, the life saving crew organized regular summer treasure hunting expeditions in which families and friends were invited to the remote island. Knowledge of the Cedar Island coin recoveries would probably have been lost in history had it not been for a report compiled for the Virginia Coast Reserve. A researcher recorded the stories of the coin recoveries in interviews with some of the last of the oldtimers.

Cedar Island makes one wonder about the other similar barrier islands along this remote section of coast. Very few of these beaches have ever been thoroughly worked with modern metal detectors and it is quite possible that other coin beaches, unkown and never searched, are waiting to be found.

CHAPTER 21
The Sinking of the Merida

By 1911, steamers, with their vastly greater reliability and
safety, had replaced sailing vessels in most areas of maritime
commerce. The mid-Atlantic lifesaving stations maintained their
readiness and vigilance as coastal traffic grew always heavier,
but fewer times each year were they called into action to aid
grounded vessels.

Typical of the steamers of this era were the *Merida* and the
Admiral Farragut. The five-year-old *Merida* was the flagship of
the Ward Line's New York and Cuba Steamship Company. With
a length of 400 feet, three decks fore and aft, steel bulkheaded
construction, and two enormous steam engines developing 5,000
horsepower, she was the favorite of regular New York–Havana
passengers, and made that run in only seventy-two hours while
cruising at nineteen knots. Just after midnight on May 12, 1911,
the *Merida* was northbound through a dense fog about fifty miles
off the Virginia Capes. She was only ten hours out of New York,
about to complete a voyage that had begun in Vera Cruz and
Progreso, Mexico, three days earlier.

The thirteen-year-old *Admiral Farragut* was smaller at 291 feet
and two decks fore and aft. Like most steamers of this period, she
had two fore and aft schooner rigged masts and was equipped
with the new wireless apparatus. Just after midnight on May 12,
the *Admiral Farragut,* like the *Merida,* was fifty miles off the
Virginia Capes. She was outbound from Philadelphia, cutting
through heavy fog at thirteen knots and bound for Kingston,
Jamaica.

Both ships were "running on the horn," that is, proceeding at
near normal speed while announcing their presence with regular
blasts on their foghorns. At 12:30 A.M., the officers and crewmen manning both bridges found themselves staring helplessly at

a terrifying sight. Following the confusing echo of another fog-horn, a few lights became visible, then the dark mass of another ship materialized out of the foggy night. In seconds it was over. At a combined speed of nearly thirty knots, the steel bow of the *Admiral Farragut* rammed the *Merida,* knifing fifteen feet through plates and bulkheads amidships. Almost immediately after the terrible shock of the collision, the *Merida* was plunged into darkness, her engines and generators disabled. She began taking water and settling into a starboard list. The *Admiral Farragut,* with her bows stove in and a gaping hole at her waterline, drifted off into the darkness. At first it was thought that she, too, might be in danger of sinking, but her forward bulkheads held.

Fortunately, the sea was calm and the boats quickly transferred 320 people from the *Merida* to the *Admiral Farragut.* Only a handful of officers remained aboard the *Merida* as her bow settled deeper into the Atlantic. The leaking and now overloaded *Admiral Farragut* rode fearfully low in the water herself as crews worked feverishly to repair the wireless rigging which had come down in the collision. At 5:15 A.M., the Captain of the *Merida* was the last man to be taken off. Fifteen minutes later, he watched from a boat as his ship raised her stern nearly perpendicular and slid beneath the waves. At the same time, the *Admiral Farragut*'s

The S.S. *Merida,* sunk in a collision with the S.S. *Admiral Farragut* in 1911, about forty-five miles off the Virginia Capes. The wreck, with millions in Mexican silver and personal jewelry aboard, has been the object of treasure salvage expeditions almost since the day it sank. Courtesy Mariners' Museum, Newport News, VA.

wireless became operative and the first distress signals were sent. Replies came almost immediately from the steamer *Hamilton* and the battleship U.S.S. *Iowa*. By 8:00 A.M., the *Hamilton* had taken aboard all passengers for safe delivery to Norfolk and the *Iowa* began escorting the *Admiral Farragut* on a slow five knot voyage to a New York dry dock.

The sinking of the *Merida* was front page news across the country and a loss of one million dollars was estimated for both the ship and her cargo. Only a few days later there was renewed interest when the *Norfolk Beacon* reported that "seventeen tons of bar silver," being transferred from Mexican banks to U.S. repositories, had also gone down with the ship. Other sources confirmed the loss of the silver cargo which was then valued at $500,000. Such a shipment was not unusual for, in those years, Mexico was rocked by revolution and the government, banks, and citizens shipped much wealth out of the country to keep it out of the hands of insurrectionists. The passengers included many very wealthy Mexicans who lost personal fortunes in gold and jewels.

Two weeks after the sinking, a New York newspaper raised the value of the silver aboard to one million dollars. The *Norfolk Beacon* then doubled that. If the *Merida* needed any more reason to confirm its title as a treasure ship, it came quickly in the form of wild rumors that Mexican agents had smuggled aboard nothing less than the crown jewels of Emperor Maximilian for eventual return to the Austrian Hapsburgs. Those jewels alone, so the rumors claimed, were worth five million dollars.

The *Merida* had rested on the bottom in two hundred feet of water only three short months when the first salvage attempt was announced. A Norfolk diver and salvage man, Captain Charles Williamson, president of the Williamson Submarine Corporation, was to use his "submarine tube caisson" for the attempt. Williamson's device was a one-yard-diameter, reinforced, airtight tube fitted with an airlock on the surface and a large working turret on the bottom. Divers would descend to the turret on an internal ladder. From there, with the benefit of internal and external electric lights, they would manipulate external mechanical arms to perform the actual salvage work. The great advantage, Williamson claimed, was that divers could work at depth while under normal air pressure. The concept of the device was advanced for the period, but actual use of the bulky equipment in high seas conditions was impractical. No more was heard from Captain Williamson.

The barnacles at last had time to grow on the hull of the *Merida,* but the treasure wreck was not forgotten. After two early attempts failed, the *Merida* was back on the front page of the *New York Times* on October 1, 1924.

Expedition Sails Today to Seek Treasure Worth $3,000,000 on Bed of Ocean 14 Years

A third expedition which hopes to recover $3,000,000 in gold, silver, and precious stones, which have been at the bottom of the Atlantic Ocean for fourteen years is expected to sail today from the Tebo Yacht Basin plant of the Todd Shipyards Corporation, off Twenty-third Street, South Brooklyn.

The expedition will leave on two steam trawlers, the Foam and the Spray. A group of well known New York business and society men are behind the project. They include Franklin I. Mallory, W. Heyward Drayton III, Anthony J. Drexel Biddle, Jr., John S. Ball, and Worthington Davis.

John F. O'Hagen, a noted diver, was commissioned several weeks ago to organize the expedition. With him are Frank J. Grilley and Fredelin C. C. Neilson, former United States Navy divers, who had charge of raising the submarine F-4 which sank off Honolulu Harbor ten years ago. Each trawler carried a crew of about thirty men and a dozen of the latest models in diving suits.

The sunken treasure is all aboard the Ward Line Steamship Merida which went down sixty miles off the Virginia Capes in May, 1911, after a collision with the United Fruit Company's steamer Admiral Farragut.

The cargo of the Merida consisted of a large amount of silver, about $500,000 in gold, and many precious stones, among them the famous Maximilian rubies, once the pride of Empress Marie Charlotte, mad widow of the ill-fated ruler of Mexico.

The Merida was bound from Mexico via Havana when the collision occurred. All her passengers were saved by ships which answered her SOS calls. The vessel had 4,700 tons of copper in her hold as ballast. She is believed to be resting on an even keel on a hard sandy bottom.

The first expedition to recover the treasure was made in 1917, just before the war, when a party of New York capitalists fitted out a steamer and dragged for some days for the wreck. In 1921, the steamer Ripple, manned by a picked crew of twenty-five, with three of the best known divers in the country, was sent by another party of New York capitalists to hunt for the treasure. Both expeditions were unsuccessful.

The crews of the *Foam* and the *Spray* also failed in the face of poor late autumn weather. But the next year, the *Merida* was back in the news again, and the value of her treasure had nearly tripled during the winter.

TO RESUME TREASURE HUNT

*New Yorkers Seeking The
Sunken Merida Await
Good Weather*

PALM BEACH, Fla., Feb. 10.—The expedition which set out from New York last October to salvage $13,000,000 worth of gold and gems lost several years ago when the steamship Merida of the Ward Line sank off the Virginia Capes will resume operation before April 1, A. J. Drexel Biddle, Jr., one of the backers announced here today.

Mr. Biddle said the efforts to locate the sunken vessel were abandoned in late November because of heavy seas, which rendered the work of divers extremely hazardous. The three trawlers used by the expedition are now in Norfolk, preparing to resume operation as soon as weather permits.

After the expedition returned to the site of the *Merida* things went well and on June 30, 1925, a news article indicated success was almost at hand.

TREASURE HUNTERS EXPLORE THE MERIDA

*Divers Prepare To Cut Through Wall Of
Sunken Ship to $4,000,000 in Gold*

. . . A diver sent down from one of the trawlers has located the treasure on the sunken ship Merida. The next step will be to cut through the iron walls of the storeroom and bring up nearly thirty tons of gold and silver bullion.

Shortly after beginning to work, a storm sent the trawlers steaming to safety in Norfolk; upon their return, they found their marker buoys swept away and were unable to relocate the wreck. Several other groups publicly stated their intent to go after the treasure, and the announcements attracted particular attention in Mexico City where wealthy *Merida* survivors still hoped for recovery of their family jewels and gold. Additional salvage incentive came with a newspaper interview of the *Merida's* purser in Mexico City in 1925. Now, it seemed, the shipment of gold and silver bullion was so great that the purser's locker had to be specially reinforced to take the load.

An interesting twist to the story of the *Merida's* treasure arose in 1932, when a London fishmonger claimed the whole thing for himself. His grounds raised eyebrows all over the world, for his attorneys introduced their client, a William Brightwell, as none other than Franz Rudolph Maximilian, son of the late Emperor and his wife, the mad Empress Charlotte. The heir-apparent planned his own expedition which never left the dock, but his presence helped keep the *Merida* in the news.

The year 1933 saw action on the seabottom, on the sea over the wreck, and in courtrooms in New York and Norfolk. Attorneys sued and countersued in a confusing series of claims and counterclaims. At sea, the United States Coast Guard was asked to intervene to prevent violence and sabotage between salvage competitors at the site. In August, Captain H. L. Bowdoin, working from the vessel *Salvor,* managed to recover a small safe from the purser's office on the sunken *Merida.* The safe was brought to Norfolk amid great excitement. Captain Bowdoin, his backers, and a great crowd of curious onlookers milled about as United States Customs agents pried open the rusted safe. Inside was found only disappointment, for the sole contents were a waiter's badge, a handful of Mexican coins, and a U.S. half dollar—counterfeit at that.

One of the basic requirements of a treasure salvor is boundless optimism; to other salvors, Captain Bowdoin's failure was merely a confirmation that the Merida's treasure was intact. In 1936, a most unusual salvage vessel sailed for the wreck site. "Sailed" is a fitting term, for the *Constellation* was a 204-foot, four-masted schooner, devoid of any auxiliary power, but loaded with the best diving equipment of the day. The expedition was under the direction of Thomas P. Connally, ex-Jersey City jail warden, and now president of the Empire Marine Salvage and Engineering Company. The high point of this attempt was probably the striking picture the *Constellation* made as she sailed out of New York under full canvas bound for the Virginia Capes. This expedition never found the wreck.

The seventh major attempt on the *Merida* was made in 1937 by John D. Craig, a noted deep sea diver and prolific adventure author. Craig at least found the wreck and contributed greatly to its growing lore and legend. He announced that his *Merida* operation was a "dress rehearsal" for future work on the torpedoed *Lusitania* off England. A chapter in one of Craig's later books was devoted to the *Merida* and colorfully named "A Treasure Cursed and Double Cursed." It was lively reading and gave a detailed account of the diver-author's idea of the treasure:

> . . . Aboard the *Merida* was stowed this huge treasure of the Hapsburgs—$5,500,000 in gold, silver, and jewels, together with a consignment of 827 silver bars, originally insured in Paris and valued at $237,500. This treasure was locked in one of the two purser's safes. In the other safe was locked an additional $50,000 in gold specie and another $100,000 in like currency of various denominatons belonging to the passengers. Too, there was the famous historic pearl and ruby necklace of Charlotte—Carlotta, as the Mexicans called her—the unfortunate Empress of Maximilian, as well as the other crown jewels which had been surreptitiously smuggled out of Mexico at the last minute . . .
>
> In addition to all these valuables there was stowed in the hold of the liner some 699 bars of copper valued at $25,730, $90,000 in mahogany logs, and 6,000 tons of Jamaican rum. The officials of an American mining company, which operated in Mexico, realizing they would be looted of their mined ore by the revolutionists, placed aboard the *Merida* approximately fifteen tons of pure silver ingots. And, although it was not authenticated, it was rumored that Diaz had stored on board at Vera Cruz the famous emeralds of Quetzalcoatl . . .

Not even this fortune in Aztec and Hapsburg jewels was enough to inspire Craig to try to enter the rusting hulk, for he retired from diving and never returned. In 1938, however, the lure of the treasure attracted an expedition from Spezia, Italy.

Their equipment included several hundred dynamite bombs to blast their way into the wreck. The expedition located the *Merida* in June, re-outfitted in Norfolk, then returned for the treasure, as reported in this *New York Times* article.

Merida Salvaging To Go On

NORFOLK, Va., August 8, (AP).—The Italian salvage ship Falco, after loading supplies here, put back to sea again today to resume her attempt to salvage silver bullion from the Ward Line steamer Merida, which has been lying since May, 1911, in two hundred feet of water sixty miles off the Virginia Capes. Divers of the expedition have blasted into the Merida's strongroom and hope to begin bringing up silver bullion within the next few days.

The hurricane season discouraged long term work on the *Merida* and the *Falco* returned to Italy for the winter. In the spring of 1939, it was back over the Merida again. After a long summer of diving and blasting, the *Falco* crew, like all the others, retired empty-handed.

DROP QUEST FOR SILVER AT SEA

NORFOLK, Va., Aug. 14 (AP).—An Italian expedition which has sought for two summers to recover a $250,000 cargo of silver bullion that supposedly went down with the Ward Liner Merida off the Virginia Capes twenty-eight years ago gave up the search today. Dr. Lugi Faggian, technical director of the quest, which has cost more than $100,000 and produced only one silver ingot valued at $7.20 announced the decision to abandon operations when the salvage steamer Falco came into port. The Falco will sail for home Thursday.

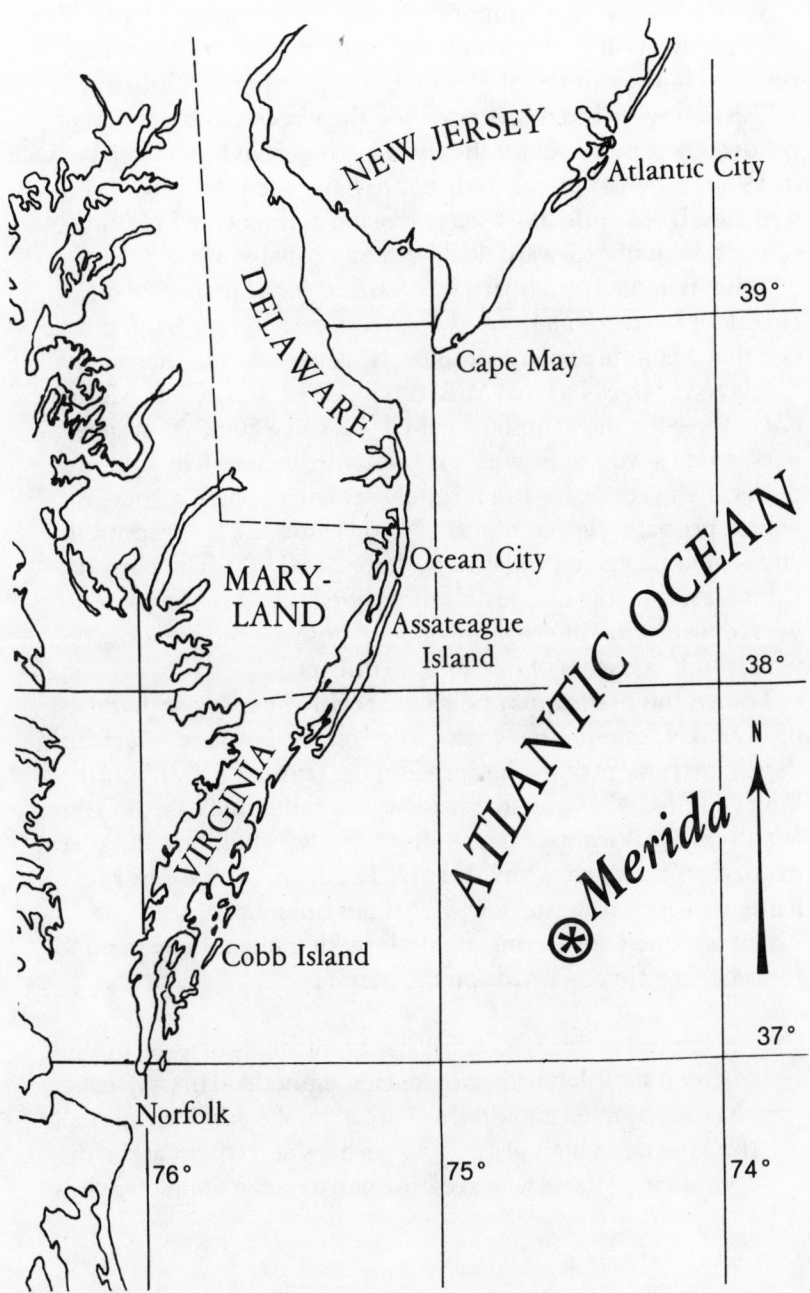

Location of the wreck site of the *Merida* at 37°20′ north latitude, 74°47′ west longitude, forty-five miles due east of Cobb Island, VA.

World War II put a temporary halt to the salvage attempts. The next known visit to the wreck was made in 1957 and reportedly resulted in the salvage of $6,000 in copper. In the 1960s and 1970s, a few SCUBA divers visited the wreck but there was no reported attempt to enter the rusted, dangerous hulk. Even back in 1938, the *Merida* was reported to have been thoroughly wrecked by the effects of sea corrosion and repeated blasting by salvors, with her forward decks already collapsed.

What is actually on board the *Merida*? Jack Horner, in his excellent book *Shipwrecks, Skin Divers, and Sunken Gold,* points out that Maximilians's crown jewels are *not,* for they are safely displayed at the National Museum in Mexico City. The Merida *did* carry—for the insurance paid it—about $500,000 in silver bars, some seven tons, which is now worth about five million dollars. The copper matte (crudely refined copper) carried as ballast probably amounted to 470 tons, not 4,700 as reported, and would be valued today at perhaps $700,000. The personal valuables, the gold and jewels of the wealthy Mexican passengers, considering the current value of gold, would certainly be worth well in excess of one million dollars.

Today, the *Merida* may be found relatively easily with the use of LORAN, satellite navigation systems, and sonar or electronic depth instruments. She lies precisely at latitude 37° 20' north, longitude 74° 47' west, about forty-five miles due east of Cobb Island on the Virginia eastern shore. Today's bullion values have made the *Merida* a worthy treasure target and, some day, her name will appear in the news headlines once again.

But anyone considering the undertaking might keep in mind John Craig's closing words on the *Merida:*

> . . . For today the *Merida* still lies grotesquely dressed in a suit of green shell and brown barnacles, embedded in twelve feet of sand—cursed and double cursed by the guardian spirits of the long dead high priest who perhaps still laughs at the discomfiture of those who seek the ghostly relic's hidden riches.

PART VI

Mid-Atlantic
Treasure Today

CHAPTER 22
Modern Treasure Salvage

Treasure salvage is nothing new, for man's attempts to recover his lost treasures have been going on since the first ships sank. His early successes were few, not for lack of desire or effort, but rather for the crude search and recovery techniques that limited his effectiveness.

In September, 1798, when the British naval salvage ships sought the *deBraak*, they finally located the shallow water wreck with the only technique known at the time—dragging with hooks hoping to snag timbers or rigging. Wreck location relied upon those same primitive techniques well into the 1900s. Of the many expeditions that sought the huge, four hundred-foot-long hulk of the *Merida*, half were unable even to locate the wreck. Without electronic navigation or detection instruments, and working far beyond any landmarks, simply returning to a previously located site was a challenge. Celestial navigation computations could return one to within one-half mile of a high seas position, but in deep water or poor visibility, locating the wreck was still largely a matter of luck. When Simon Lake was within a few hundred feet of the *Hussar*, his search technique was limited to sounding with wooden pilings hoping to strike timbers in the riverbottom silt. And 1,400 silver bars were knowingly left in the mud of the Arthur Kill, simply because there was no way to precisely locate them.

Even after a treasure was located, the technology to assure its recovery did not exist. Prior to the 1880s, sustained underwater work was possible only with clumsy diving bells with their non-replenishable air supplies. The introduction of reliable mechanical air compressors finally made possible "hard hat" diving equipment; this familiar, bulky outfit was a prop for a hundred "B" movies and the mainstay of salvage divers until

SCUBA (self-contained underwater breathing apparatus) arrived in the early 1950s. Unlike hard hat, SCUBA was relatively inexpensive and portable, required little in the way of surface support, and put many shipwrecks within reach of the individual diver rather than just expeditions or large companies.

The advent of the modern treasure salvage era followed the commercial availability of SCUBA. Treasure recoveries were a rarity in hard hat days but, by 1960, they had become almost commonplace. Most occurred in Florida or the Caribbean, where history readily confirmed the presence of galleon wrecks. In many areas of the tropics there was little sand shoaling and the hard coral seabottom left wreck sites visible to the trained eyes of treasure salvors. Clear, warm water and a pleasant climate encouraged year-round work. Anyone with SCUBA, a small boat, and some enthusiasm was a potential treasure salvor. After the obvious wreck sites had been exploited, the salvors turned to technology to locate others, and the resultant development and improvement of search and recovery techniques have at last brought about the capability to work many mid-Atlantic wrecks.

The first attempts of treasure salvors to detect the unseen electronically came with experimental use of underwater models of early metal detectors following World War II. Success eluded most treasure hunters, for the wreck site metal was often buried deeper than the limited range of the early instruments. The biggest breakthrough in wreck location came not with detectors, but with improved versions of the magnetometers first employed by the U.S. Navy to locate underwater naval mines during World War II. After the War, magnetometers found immediate commercial application in geophysical prospecting for oil and mineral bodies and in marine construction to locate pipelines and cables.

By 1960, the bulky magnetometers of the war years had been refined into the "mag" of today, a light, portable, highly sensitive instrument, with many models adapted specifically to marine use. Typical of advances in electronic technology, as sophistication and efficiency increased, costs decreased to make the instruments available to almost anyone. While the mags do not respond to the presence of gold, silver, copper, brass, or other non-magnetic metals, they do reveal the anomalies in the earth's magnetic field created by the local presence of ferrous metals. In the world of the treasure salvor, this translated to the anchors, cannon, and shipboard iron fittings that are found on most early wreck sites.

The mags employed by modern treasure salvors are suitcase-sized instruments attached by cable to a sensing head which is towed underwater behind a small survey boat. The locations of anomalies are quickly marked with weighted buoys. Divers then check the bottom, excavating, if necessary, to reveal the source of the anomaly. An actual magnetometer survey, especially one in an area of heavy marine use such as the mid-Atlantic, can be extremely frustrating; the bottom will be littered with metal debris, plates, anchors, chain, and a thousand other rusted re-minders of the passage of thousands of ships. Still, mags have been vital in locating most of the treasure wreck sites salvaged today.

Side-scan sonar is another instrument treasure salvors have found useful in wreck location surveys. Basically a recording sonar transmitter-receiver, "side-scan" literally draws a picture of unusual and unnatural shapes on the seabottom, such as that of a wreck. Salvors have also benefitted from sub-bottom profilers, which detect and record variations in the density of the sub-seabottom, revealing the presence of unusual materials, such as wood or steel, which often indicate a wreck site. Technology has given modern salvors an enormous advantage over their prede-cessors; side-scan sonar easily locate wrecks such as the *Merida*, and sub-bottom profilers would be invaluable in pinpointing the silver bars that lie buried in the mud of the Arthur Kill.

While these devices are more attuned to the professional or commercial salvage field, instruments also exist for individual use that greatly facilitate searches of the mid-Atlantic coin beaches. Metal detectors originated in the 1930s, when experimentation with radio direction-finding equipment showed a measureable response to distant metal objects. From this discovery came the introduction of the bulky land mine detectors employed exten-sively by the Army in World War II.

The operation of mine detectors was based upon the principle of electrical induction; that is, that any conductor, which includes all metals, will establish an electro-magnetic field when charged. A detector was both a transmitter and a receiver, emitting the radio signal necessary to induce current in a distant metallic object, then detecting the resulting electromagnetic field. The early mine detectors, the forerunners of our modern metal detectors, were clumsy and required heavy battery power sources. With a rather limited range, they were effective only on larger objects.

After the war, hobbyists were seen strapped into the strange

156 · *Mid-Atlantic Treasure Today*

contraptions walking the beaches, receiving smiles and condescending nods from observers. In the 1950s, basic electrical components remained the same, but commercial manufacturers began producing lighter, more sensitive instruments. Introduction of the transistor brought a great reduction in size and weight, and competitive research between manufacturers has resulted in the highly sensitive and sophisticated instruments of today. Modern detectors incorporate state-of-the-art electronic concepts and components, as well as innovative human engineering features.

Many detectors are designed specifically for "coin shooting" and feature a variety of interchangeable sensing heads, some designed for underwater use. Many instruments have "discriminating" circuitry, useful in differentiating quickly between objects of value, such as coins, and common metal trash. The disturbing effects of mineral salts may now be tuned out, thus making the detectors well suited for use on salt beaches. There is little similarity between the early detectors and the instruments available today. The best commercial models are now so sophisticated that their overall effectiveness is no longer dependent upon the inherent capability of the instrument, but rather upon the operator's ability to make full use of the many features.

At a cost of about four hundred dollars each, quality detectors take much of the luck out of searching the mid-Atlantic coin beaches. A single silver Spanish silver pillar dollar would pay for the detector, and a gold coin, regardless of condition, would pay for it many times over.

Another aspect of treasure that was largely ignored in early salvage days, but which has assumed considerable importance today, is research. The era of the "pie in the sky" approach is over; most knowledgeable backers, prior to committing the considerable capital to fund a modern expedition, insist upon seeing documentation proving the treasure does indeed exist. Research in libraries and archives can be nearly as exciting as salvage itself. Maritime historical sources may be found in local and university libraries, historical societies, and museums. Several excellent books dealing specifically with shipwrecks, treasure, and salvage are available. Two of the best that have become standards of reference, both in historical and technical areas, are Robert Marx's *Shipwrecks of the Western Hemisphere* and John S. Potter's *The Treasure Diver's Guide*.

CHAPTER 23
The Eternal Lure of Treasure

Twenty-five years ago, a retired building contractor named Kip Wagner found blackened pieces of eight on the beaches north of Fort Pierce, Florida. He continued to search and his desire to locate the source of the silver coins eventually led to the discovery of the wreck sites of the 1715 Spanish treasure fleet. This brought one of the first great recoveries of the modern treasure salvage era; the media gave it full coverage and the public received its first exposure to successful modern treasure salvage, the history behind it, and the adventure of doing it. The lure of treasure was enormous, both to passive observers and to a growing legion of active adventurers who began to participate in it themselves. Since Kip Wagner found those first pieces of eight on that Florida beach, there has been more treasure salvage activity than ever before.

Modern treasure salvage is just making its appearance along the mid-Atlantic coast. During the 1960s and 1970s, when the Florida and Caribbean wrecks were giving up millions, mid-Atlantic treasure remained forgotten, hidden under silt and shoals, or resting in water too deep to permit easy salvage. The image of the mid-Atlantic treasure hunter was a weekend SCUBA diver who contented himself with bringing back brass portholes and deck fittings. But these are the 1980s, and two things have happened to make mid-Atlantic treasure salvage a reality. First is the availability of the technology needed to locate, reach, and work the wrecks. Second is the spectacular recent rise in the value of sunken treasure, which more than offsets the high cost of the operational technology. Dramatically increased bullion, numismatic, and artifact values of sunken treasure have transformed the "million dollar" wreck of 1870 into the ten million dollar wreck of today.

During the summer of 1981, mid-Atlantic treasure salvage made national news. In a portent of the future, a diving team used saturation diving techniques and subsea habitats to successfully enter the wreck of the *Andrea Doria,* recovering a safe which, as of this writing, has yet to be opened. If the *Andrea Doria* can be worked in 190 feet of water, so can the nearby *Republic,* lying only a bit deeper at 240 feet, with its fortune in gold coinage. And so can the *Merida* with its millions in silver bars and personal jewelry. For nearly eight decades, the seven tons of silver in the Arthur Kill was not worth going after. Now that it is worth well in excess of ten million dollars, at least three groups, each armed with the research and technology necessary, are fighting in the courts to win the right of being first salvor.

Not that long ago, the thought that Spanish treasure galleons might be wrecked on the mid-Atlantic coast was discounted as legend. Today, there is a half-million dollar expedition backed by European research and the best electronic technology seeking the wrecks of the 1750 Spanish treasure fleet off the Eastern Shore. In 1980, I was fortunate to see firsthand the recovery of English gold guineas from the wreck of the *Faithful Steward* off Delaware.

And what of those wrecks where the existence of real treasure might be argued? The H.M.S. *Hussar* and the H.M.S. *deBraak* have been the target of a legion of salvage attempts, yet solid proof does not exist confirming the belief that there is one bit of treasure aboard either of those celebrated wrecks. But—neither have any salvors confirmed there isn't, which seems to be the more important point. Simon Lake, in the middle of his four-year attempt on the *Hussar,* readily admitted his uncertainty as to the existence of the treasure, saying, "It is not the gold so much as the satisfaction of solving the riddle, 'though some gold would do no harm."

Lake was acknowledging the existence of a reward of a different sort, one of adventure, of challenge, and of the close association with history that is a major part of every quest for treasure. Adventure, by its definition, involves risk, and every serious quest for treasure will risk something, whether physical or financial. Rest assured there will be a challenge, for if a treasure were so easy to recover, it wouldn't be there today. The reward most difficult to explain to those who have not sought for sunken treasure is the association with history. When it is *your* hand that reaches out to touch treasures and artifacts lost by other men in other times, history comes alive. It is an unforgettable, and quite possibly addictive, experience.

All of these rewards place a very real value upon the search for treasure. Certainly, to seek for treasure is to gamble; but unlike a gaming table where there is nothing between the placing of the bet and the hopeful payoff, the quest for treasure is often greatly enriching and satisfying. In 1543, the quest for a treasure that never existed inspired one of history's greatest feats of overland exploration. Francisco Coronado opened the interior of a continent by trekking across thousands of miles of land never seen before by Europeans. No golden cities were found, for none existed, and when the expedition returned to Mexico, it was judged a failure. The journalist accompanying Coronado, however, viewed the great adventure from a different perspective and wrote: *Although they found not the gold for which they sought, better still, they found a place in which to search.*

The value of the quest has endured along with the lure of treasure itself. In 1922, Ralph D. Paine, in his *Book of Buried Treasure*, expressed the same thought again.

> Faith, imagination, and a vigorous physique comprise the essential equipment of a treasure seeker. Capital is desired, but not absolutely necessary, for it would be hard indeed to find a neighborhood in which some legend or other of buried gold is not current. If one is unable to finance an expedition aboard a swift, black-hulled schooner, it is always possible to dig for the treasure of poor Captain Kidd and it is really a matter of small importance that he left no treasure in his wake. The zest of the game is in the seeking.

Mid-Atlantic treasure hunters may now look forward both to the rewards of the quest and, perhaps, the treasures themselves. The treasures are as real as the history of the coast, for they are its direct legacy. A fortunate few will enjoy the rare experience of diving to an ancient shipwreck and clearing away the sands of the centuries to uncover bars of gold or silver. All of us will be able to relive their adventures in books to come. Others of us—again, the fortunate—will walk a mid-Atlantic beach after a northeast storm and pick from the sand a piece of eight or a pillar dollar. And on that coin will be the words of classic treasure, *Hispana et Indies Rex—King of Spain and the Indies*—the sound of which will make us look seaward . . . to ponder the rest of it.

Index